I ♥ CHEESE

a cookbook

I ♥ CHEESE

a cookbook

60 Ooey, Gooey, Delicious Meals
for Serious Cheese Lovers

MIHAELA METAXA-ALBU

Chef and Founder of Blondelish.com

PAGE STREET
PUBLISHING CO.

PAGE STREET
PUBLISHING CO.

Copyright © 2020 Mihaela Metaxa-Albu

First published in 2020 by
Page Street Publishing Co.
27 Congress Street, Suite 105
Salem, MA 01970
www.pagestreetpublishing.com

Distributed by Macmillan, sales in Canada by The Canadian Manda Group.

24 23 22 21 20   1 2 3 4 5

ISBN-13: 978-1-64567-180-0
ISBN-10: 1-64567-180-1

Library of Congress Control Number: 2019957330

Cover and book design by Ashley Tenn for Page Street Publishing Co.
Photography by YumCreative.com

Printed and bound in China

I dedicate this book to my husband, who's been part of my cooking journey since the beginning. By the time I finished this book, he was ready to start a career as a professional food taster, as he literally tried all of my recipes . . . sometimes more than once. Thanks for your love and support along the way!

♥

CONTENTS

STILTON, ROQUEFORT & GORGONZOLA

GOUDA, GRUYÈRE, CHEDDAR, HALLOUMI & PROVOLONE

PARMIGIANO-REGGIANO, GRANA PADANO & PECORINO ROMANO
Rich, Savory Meals with Decadent Hard-Grating Cheeses

MIX & MATCH
Delicious, Flavorful Combos of Different Cheeses and Textures

INTRODUCTION

"I'll bring the cheese; you bring the wine."
—Mihaela Metaxa-Albu (aka "Blondelish")

Hey cheese lovers,

Before diving into these mouth-watering recipes, I'd like to say a few words about the story behind this book and what you can expect to find.

I am Mihaela Metaxa-Albu, chef and photographer at Blondelish.com. About ten years ago, when I was living in Bucharest, I fell in love and, as our relationship grew, we started spending more evenings at home enjoying romantic cuddles and pizza. Even though I enjoyed pizza, I realized that this wasn't a very romantic dinner—and not that healthy, either. So, I decided to bring some variety to our eating habits, and that's when I started cooking.

As you might imagine, I was terrible at it in the beginning. But for some reason I'm still trying to figure out, my boyfriend loved the new direction I was taking with our meals and he encouraged me to pursue my newfound passion. Being crazy in love probably helped a lot, too.

I started cooking more elaborate dinners, and then I dove into making lunches and breakfasts. Before too long, we moved to London so I could study culinary arts at Southgate College. After completing my courses, I landed a job as a pastry chef at Zuma London and later, I went on to work at Ottolenghi.

I don't think my boyfriend was expecting this when he encouraged me to pursue my passion! Fortunately, he became my husband, and even though we were both living with hectic schedules, we still enjoyed our romantic home-cooked dinners and always tried to come up with new dishes and meal ideas.

One day, as we were strolling through Borough Market, we stumbled upon a cheese store that boasted many types of cheese from all over the world. After a few tastings, we decided to make a cheese board for our romantic weekend dinner and pile it with all sorts of cheese. That dinner was the moment we both fell in love with cheese. It wasn't that we hadn't tried cheese before, but until then, our selections were limited to only the most available varieties.

An extra-full cheese board became a staple dish for our weekend dinners. Soon enough, I started wondering what else I could cook with my new favorite ingredient. I started experimenting and tweaking classic recipes by adding different types of cheese. Without being aware of it at the time, that was the incipient moment of this book.

Of course, not all of my dishes came out great, and it took time to perfect recipes with cheeses that go well for breakfast, lunch, dinner and dessert. Luckily, I jotted down my successes, and now I am happy to share them with my fellow cheese lovers in this book you are holding.

I Heart Cheese is an expression of my love for cheese in all of its forms. It has 60 cheese-based recipes for every meal, all prominently featuring some type of cheese. The recipes explored in this book include textures from fresh, soft and hard cheeses. They also explore different flavors, from extra mild to super pungent.

Best of all, the recipes in *I Heart Cheese* are incredibly easy to follow, as are all of my recipes on Blondelish.com. They're perfect for showing off on special occasions and gatherings, such as birthdays and Christmas, but they're also wonderful for simple daily meals, enabling you to satiate the appetites of all cheese lovers. Furthermore, the recipes in this book range from soups to pasta, from salads to cakes and much more. You'll find cheese in places you never expected to see it before, bringing powerful new flavors to longstanding dishes.

Apart from being an expression of my love for cheese, I also consider this work an homage to its history and the multitude of ways that cheese is incorporated into cuisines everywhere. Whether it's French Camembert, Dutch Gouda, English Cheddar or American Monterey Jack, you will surely find your favorite here.

Moreover, these recipes will fit most budgets. If you're on a tight one, you can make them with the usual cheese brands from your local grocery store. If you can afford to spend more, you can indulge in the more flavorful aged cheeses from specialty cheese shops.

Heck, if your budget allows, you can go nuts with regional aged cheeses—such as Pecorino Toscano PDO Aged instead of the usual Pecorino Romano or XXX-tra Sharp 18-Month Aged Cheddar (handcrafted in New York) instead of the usual English Cheddar—or splurge on Valdeón Blue Cheese ICP (from Spain) or Traditional Dutch Red Wax Gouda.

Another interesting find that I recommend trying is Cambozola from Germany, which is a seductively rich and intense combo of Camembert and Gorgonzola. It can be used in recipes such as Roasted Red Pepper and Tomato Soup with Gorgonzola Piccante (page 68) or Twice-Baked Butternut Squash with Gorgonzola (page 72).

I Heart Cheese aims to make cheese digestible for everybody, both literally and in terms of knowledge. This book will inspire you to try new things and to get more creative with your everyday dishes. The goal is to educate, inform and inspire foodies with delicious ways to incorporate cheese into your cooking by using these recipes as shining examples of the power of cheese in the kitchen.

I hope you enjoy this book . . . and don't forget the wine.

♥

BURRATA, MOZZARELLA, RICOTTA & CREAM CHEESE

Creamy Meals with Mild Yet Addictive Fresh Cheese

Perhaps the most mild-flavored type of cheese, fresh cheese makes up for it with rich and creamy texture. There are many types of fresh cheese, but it is always the most delicate and smooth, due to it being the youngest form of cheese, undergoing no aging processes. While you wouldn't substitute ricotta or mozzarella cheese for Parmesan, fresh cheeses certainly have a time and place where they are the superior type to use. They are easy to make at home (see the recipes on pages 30 to 37) and are often the most affordable cheeses to buy.

One of the most popular fresh cheeses is mozzarella. Made by heating cheese curds and stretching them, it has a moist and creamy texture, with a mild, dairy-like flavor. In its chilled form, mozzarella has very little give when you bite into it, making it a great ingredient to serve in large chunks for salads or cold appetizers, such as my Citrusy Fennel and Burrata Salad (page 21). When heated, the cheese melts like no other, providing richness and a wonderfully gooey texture. Burrata is mozzarella's fancier cousin and consists of a ball of fresh mozzarella filled with rich cream and curds of cheese. It makes a great show-stopping ingredient all on its own, so try tearing balls of burrata and folding them into piping-hot Burrata and Roasted Tomato Pasta (page 17).

Ricotta is extremely versatile, making a great ingredient not only in savory foods, but in desserts as well. It's also very easy to make at home, as you'll find in my recipe for rich, whole-milk Homemade Ricotta Cheese (page 34). With a creamy, spoonable consistency, it contains small curds running throughout the cheese and has a very smooth flavor. The light texture provides the essential fluffiness found in my Chocolate Chip Ricotta Pancakes (page 18).

Whether you use rich and tangy cream cheese to whip up a quick batch of No-Bake Berry Cheesecake Jars (page 22) or ooey gooey mozzarella in our melty Pancetta-Wrapped Grilled Cheese Sandwich (page 14), you'll quickly learn that fresh cheese isn't just for spreading on bagels.

PANCETTA-WRAPPED GRILLED CHEESE SANDWICH

The combination of gooey mozzarella cheese and salty pancetta makes a simple grilled cheese sandwich taste absolutely divine. This version of the classic is encased in a crispy cured pork layer, creating the perfect exterior all the way around. A good amount of garlic and fresh herbs give the cheesy filling tons of flavor that you'll be craving. The salty pancetta and rich cheese can be served with a crisp white wine, such as a Pinot Grigio.

PREP TIME: 10 minutes | **COOK TIME:** 8 minutes | **MAKES** 4 servings

MEAL: Breakfast, Lunch, Dinner

¼ cup (57 g) salted butter, softened

1 large clove garlic, minced or finely grated

Kosher salt and freshly ground black pepper, to taste

Small handful of fresh parsley, chopped

Small handful of fresh oregano, center stems removed and leaves finely chopped

Small handful of fresh mint leaves, chopped

8 slices of white bread

14 oz (397 g) mozzarella cheese, shredded

12 thin slabs of pancetta, cut in half lengthwise

1. In a small bowl, add the butter, garlic and a pinch of salt and pepper. Mix well and set aside.

2. In another small bowl, combine the parsley, oregano and mint. Set aside.

3. Using a butter knife, evenly spread the butter mixture on one side of each slice of bread.

4. On a work surface, lay out 4 of the bread slices with the buttered side facing down. Add equal amounts of the mozzarella cheese to each slice. Generously sprinkle the herb mixture over the cheese and season with salt and pepper to taste.

5. Top with the remaining bread slices, buttered side up, to create four sandwiches.

6. Preheat a large skillet or stove-top grill pan over medium heat. Take one sandwich and wrap it with 6 slices of pancetta. Repeat with the remaining three sandwiches.

7. When the skillet is hot, add the sandwiches, placing the side where the pancetta slices meet facing down. Cooking this side first will allow the pancetta slices to get crispy and stay firmly on the sandwiches. Cook for 3 to 4 minutes, or until the cheese starts to melt.

8. Use the back of a spatula to gently press down on the top of each sandwich. Flip each sandwich over and continue to cook for another 3 to 4 minutes, until the cheese is completely melted and the sandwich is golden-brown on both sides.

BURRATA AND ROASTED TOMATO PASTA

Creamy burrata cheese is the secret weapon to making any dish instantly irresistible. On the outside, it looks like a ball of fresh mozzarella, but as soon as it's torn open, it reveals a center of rich cream and curds of delicious cheese. Roasting the cherry tomatoes concentrates their sweetness, releasing all of their flavorful juices. With only a handful of ingredients, this dish is surprisingly easy to make. The pop of red from the cherry tomatoes and creamy burrata transform it into something awe-inspiring. The milkiness of the burrata and sweet acidity of the tomatoes provide a perfect pairing for light to medium-bodied reds, such as Côtes du Rhôn.

PREP TIME: 10 minutes | **COOK TIME:** 25 minutes | **MAKES** 4 servings

MEAL: Lunch, Dinner

12 oz (340 g) mixed cherry tomatoes

2 tbsp (30 ml) olive oil

3 cloves garlic, minced or grated

Sea salt and freshly ground black pepper, to taste

12½ oz (354 g) of long cut pasta (e.g. tagliatelle)

3 tbsp (45 g) salted butter

8 oz (226 g) fresh burrata cheese, torn into pieces

Large handful of fresh basil leaves

Fresh thyme or other herbs of choice (e.g., dill, parsley or basil)

1. Preheat the oven to 400°F (200°C).

2. In a mixing bowl, add the tomatoes, olive oil, garlic and a generous sprinkle of salt and pepper. Toss gently, making sure the tomatoes are well coated.

3. Transfer the tomatoes to a rimmed sheet pan and place it on the lower rack of the oven.

4. Roast for 12 to 15 minutes, or until the tomatoes are lightly charred and burst.

5. In the meantime, bring a large pot of salted water to a boil. Add the pasta and cook until al dente, tender yet firm to the bite, according to the package directions.

6. Drain the pasta and add the butter. Toss with a pair of tongs until the butter is melted and the pasta is nicely coated.

7. When the cherry tomatoes are done, remove from the oven and scatter them over the pasta, including all the juices from the pan.

8. Add the burrata cheese and fresh herbs. Gently toss to combine. Grind some pepper over the pasta and sprinkle with salt to taste.

TIP: *Use any long cut pasta you want (e.g., spaghetti, angel hair pasta, tagliatelle, fettuccine or linguine) and remember to cook it al dente. Al dente is an Italian term that literally means "to the tooth." It refers to the texture of cooked pasta that is neither crunchy nor too soft, making it the perfect texture that appeals to the teeth.*

CHOCOLATE CHIP RICOTTA PANCAKES

Ricotta pancakes are the cream of the crop in the world of griddle cakes.
Nothing gives pancakes a fluffy, cloud-like texture quite like rich and creamy ricotta cheese.
Just as easy to make as traditional chocolate chip pancakes, these use Italian ricotta cheese.
The result is a batter that comes together in minutes with pancakes that will taste better than
those from your favorite restaurant. Add your favorite toppings and you'll have
a truly decadent treat for breakfast or a unique dessert.

PREP TIME: 10 minutes | **COOK TIME:** 35–45 minutes | **MAKES** about 6 servings
MEAL: Breakfast, Dessert

2 large eggs

1½ cups (360 ml) milk

⅓ cup (40 g) powdered sugar

8 oz (226 g) whole milk ricotta cheese

1½ tsp (8 ml) vanilla extract

1½ tsp (3 g) orange zest

2 cups (250 g) all-purpose flour

1 tsp baking powder

½ tsp baking soda

Pinch of sea salt

¾ cup (126 g) chocolate chips

Coconut oil cooking spray

TOPPING SUGGESTIONS

Honey, butter, maple syrup, agave syrup, walnuts, pecans, hazelnuts

1. In a medium bowl, combine the eggs with the milk, sugar, ricotta cheese, vanilla and orange zest. Whisk until well combined.

2. In a large bowl, sift the flour and add the baking powder, baking soda and salt. Stir lightly to combine.

3. Gradually whisk the ricotta mixture into the dry ingredients until a smooth batter is formed. Gently fold in the chocolate chips.

4. Heat a large nonstick skillet over medium heat. Lightly spray with coconut oil.

5. Pour in about ⅓ cup (80 ml) of the batter. Cook for 2 to 3 minutes or until bubbles appear on the surface. Gently flip the pancake over and cook for 1 to 2 minutes longer. Remove the pancake from the skillet and set aside on a plate. Repeat with the remaining batter and cover the cooked pancakes as you go to keep them warm.

6. Divide the pancakes and stack them on individual plates. Add the toppings of your choice.

TIP: *For this recipe, you can use the homemade ricotta cheese from page 34.*

CITRUSY FENNEL AND BURRATA SALAD

Fresh burrata cheese really shines when it's allowed to take on the flavor of zesty citrus fruits such as grapefruit and orange. In this light, summery salad, greens are tossed with chunks of creamy burrata, refreshingly crisp fennel slices, segmented citrus and a vinaigrette that will awaken the senses. This healthy salad is the perfect balance between richly satisfying and pleasantly light. Serve with low-acidity white wines, such as Chardonnay, or fruity reds, such as Grenache.

PREP TIME: 25 minutes | **MAKES** 4-6 servings

MEAL: Appetizer, Side Dish

DRESSING

¼ cup (60 ml) extra virgin olive oil

1 tbsp (15 ml) orange juice, freshly squeezed

1 tbsp (15 ml) lemon juice, freshly squeezed

1 tbsp (15 ml) white wine vinegar

1 small shallot, minced or grated on a microplane

1 tsp chili flakes, or to taste

½ tsp dried herbs de Provence

Salt and freshly ground black pepper, to taste

SALAD

2 large fennel bulbs, thinly sliced

1 pink grapefruit, peeled, pith removed and cut into segments

1 large orange, peeled, pith removed and cut into segments

2 handfuls fresh leafy greens of choice

16 oz (454 g) burrata cheese, drained and roughly torn into bite-size pieces

Salt and freshly ground back pepper, to taste

1. To make the dressing, in a small jar, add all of the dressing ingredients. Screw the lid on tightly and shake vigorously to emulsify.

2. To prepare the fennel, trim the bottom of the bulbs, then cut the bulbs in half lengthwise and peel off any wilted outer layers. Using a very sharp knife, thinly slice the fennel crosswise.

3. In a mixing bowl, add the fennel slices with the grapefruit and orange segments. Pour in the dressing and gently toss to combine. Refrigerate for at least 30 minutes.

4. When ready to serve, add in the greens and give the salad a good toss to coat with the dressing. Top with the torn pieces of fresh burrata and season with salt and freshly ground black pepper, if needed.

NO-BAKE BERRY CHEESECAKE JARS

Cheesecake is a wildly popular dessert, and for good reason. Rich and tangy sweetened cream cheese, crisp biscuits and tart fresh berries make these no-bake cheesecake jars irresistibly delicious. I used whipped cream with cream cheese for a super fluffy texture. Embarrassingly simple to throw together, they are perfect for an easy summer dessert or a special-occasion breakfast.

PREP TIME: 15 minutes | **MAKES** 4–5 servings

MEAL: Breakfast, Dessert

1½ cups (360 ml) whipping cream

⅓ cup (40 g) powdered sugar

1 tsp vanilla extract

8 oz (226 g) cream cheese, at room temperature

1¼ cups (125 g) digestive biscuits, crumbled

12 oz (340 g) mixed fresh berries, divided

1. Place the whipping cream, sugar and vanilla in a mixing bowl and whisk with an electric mixer until stiff peaks form. Cover with plastic wrap and refrigerate until ready to use.

2. Place the cream cheese in another mixing bowl and beat with an electric mixer until smooth and softened. Add in the whipped cream and mix on low until well combined, about 1 minute.

3. Divide the biscuits among four small jars. Add a small handful of the berries to each, reserving some for topping. Top with the cream cheese mixture.

4. Top with the remaining berries and serve immediately or refrigerate overnight.

TIP: *If you want to serve these cheesecake jars for dessert after dinner, I suggest making the cheese mixture ahead and keeping it refrigerated in an airtight container. You can store it for up to 3 days. When ready to serve, just assemble the jars. It's such a quick and satisfying dessert.*

RICOTTA COCONUT ALMOND CAKE

Fluffy ricotta cheese is the secret ingredient in this light-as-air coconut almond cake. Cakes made with nut flours can often be denser than traditional ones, but taking the time to separate the eggs and give the whites a good beating ensures that the batter will come out perfectly every time. Folding mildly creamy ricotta into the mix adds to the fluffiness and provides an addictive cloud-like texture to this summery tropical cake. Perfect for nut lovers, or those avoiding gluten, this cake is an instant crowd-pleaser.

PREP TIME: 15 minutes | **COOK TIME:** 50 minutes | **MAKES** about 8 servings
MEAL: Snack, Dessert

¼ cup (57 g) butter, softened

¾ cup (150 g) coconut sugar

1 vanilla bean, split and seeds scraped

1 tbsp (3 g) lime zest

4 eggs, yolks and whites separated, at room temperature, divided

1 cup (246 g) ricotta cheese

1¾ cups (166 g) almond meal

½ cup (68 g) coconut flour

1 tsp apple cider vinegar

2–3 tbsp (30–45 g) sliced almonds

2–3 tbsp (30–45 g) coconut flakes

1. Heat the oven to 325°F (163°C). Line the base and sides of an 8 x 2½–inch (20 x 6.5–cm) round cake pan with parchment paper and set aside.

2. Place the butter, sugar, vanilla bean seeds and lime zest in a large mixing bowl and whisk with an electric mixer for 5 to 6 minutes, or until creamy.

3. Scrape down the sides of the bowl, then gradually add the egg yolks and continue to beat until fully combined.

4. Add in the ricotta cheese and mix to combine. Add the almond meal and coconut flour and beat until fully incorporated.

5. In a separate clean bowl, beat the egg whites and apple cider vinegar with an electric mixer until soft peaks form.

6. Gently fold a third of the egg whites into the cake mixture, until completely combined. Repeat with the rest of the egg whites.

7. Pour the batter into the prepared cake pan, smooth the tops with a palette knife and sprinkle with the sliced almonds and coconut flakes.

8. Cover the pan with aluminum foil and bake for 45 to 55 minutes or until cooked and firm to the touch. To test for doneness, insert a skinny bamboo skewer into the center of the cake. If it comes out clean, your cake is done and ready to remove from the oven. If not, cook for 2 to 3 minutes longer and test again.

9. Allow the cake to cool completely in the cake pan before slicing.

TIP: *If vanilla bean is difficult to source, use 1½ teaspoons (7 ml) of vanilla extract instead.*

MARINATED MOZZARELLA BALLS

Fresh mozzarella's mild flavor makes it a great candidate for marinating in your favorite herbs and spices. In this Mediterranean version, cute mozzarella pearls take an olive oil bath that's been infused with zesty flavors from sun-dried tomatoes, fresh garlic, fennel seeds, oregano and aromatic pink peppercorns. I love to eat them straight out of the jar, or serve them with bread or crackers for a flavor-packed appetizer.

PREP TIME: 5 minutes | **COOK TIME:** 2–3 minutes | **MAKES** 6 servings

MEAL: Snack, Appetizer

½ tsp fennel seeds

1 cup (240 ml) extra virgin olive oil

2–3 cloves garlic

1 tsp dried oregano

2 tsp (4 g) pink peppercorn

10½ oz (298 g) fresh mozzarella pearls or mini balls, drained

2 tbsp (30 g) dry packed sun-dried tomatoes, chopped

1. Place a heavy-based saucepan over low heat. Add the fennel seeds and cook, stirring frequently, to lightly toast them, about 1 minute.

2. Stir in the olive oil, garlic, oregano and peppercorn. Slightly warm the oil, stirring frequently, to release and infuse the flavors, for about 2 minutes. Remove from heat and allow the mixture to cool.

3. Meanwhile, place the mozzarella pearls and the sun-dried tomatoes in a large 15-ounce (425-g) jar with a lid. Pour the infused oil over the top, and gently stir to combine. Screw the lid on tightly and refrigerate until ready to serve. The cheese tastes amazing after spending at least 1 to 2 days in the infused oil and is best if used within a week.

TIPS: *Serve the mozzarella cheese balls with salad, crunchy veggies and dip or on a cheese platter. The infused oil works perfectly combined with a splash of your choice of vinegar as a dressing, so you can use it with your favorite salad.*

To make it a bit spicier, use crushed pink peppercorn instead of whole.

PESTO PASTA SALAD
WITH MOZZARELLA AND AVOCADO

Pasta salad can tend to be bland, but this one is full of flavor and texture, thanks to delicate, fresh mozzarella pearls and an herby pesto dressing. Nutty whole wheat pasta is tossed with a generous amount of mini mozzarella balls, sweet cherry tomatoes, creamy avocado, crisp cucumber and a flavorful pesto sauce. The pesto sticks to every piece of pasta and, with the large presence of creamy mozzarella, every bite is full of flavor. Be sure to make extra, because this hearty pasta salad will be the first to go at any picnic.

PREP TIME: 10 minutes | **COOK TIME:** 6–8 minutes | **MAKES** 4–5 servings
MEAL: Lunch, Dinner

8 oz (226 g) whole wheat short pasta (e.g., penne)

½ cup (120 ml) basil pesto, homemade or store-bought

2 tbsp (30 ml) freshly squeezed lemon juice

Sea salt and freshly ground black pepper, to taste

10 oz (283 g) red cherry or grape tomatoes, halved

2 ripe avocados, pitted, skins removed and diced

2 English cucumbers, cut into half moons

8 oz (226 g) fresh mozzarella pearls or mini balls, drained

1. Bring a large pot of salted water to a boil. Add the pasta and cook according to package directions. Reserve ¼ cup (60 ml) of the pasta water before draining. Drain well.

2. Stir in the pesto, lemon juice, pasta water and salt and pepper to taste. Using a wooden spoon, stir thoroughly to nicely coat the pasta.

3. Add the cherry tomatoes, avocados, cucumbers and mozzarella pearls. Toss to combine.

TIP: *If making ahead, you can refrigerate it in airtight containers for up to 48 hours.*

HOMEMADE FRESH CHEESE

Making cheese from scratch doesn't have to be complicated, and this Homemade Fresh Cheese is living proof. With only a large pot, cooking thermometer and a few other tools you probably have on hand, you can turn three cheap pantry ingredients into something awe-inspiring. After gently curdling whole milk and draining the whey from the curds, you'll find that homemade cheese really is easy peasy. The resulting cheese is reminiscent of cream cheese, with slightly less tang. Whether eating it for breakfast, spreading it on crackers, adding it to your salad or snacking on it straight from the fridge, don't be surprised if hungry loved ones gobble up this cheese in the blink of an eye.

TIME: About 15 minutes, plus inactive time to rest and drain | **MAKES** about 10 ounces (283 g)

MEAL: Breakfast, Snack, Appetizer

½ gallon (1.9 L) whole milk

¼ cup (60 ml) white or cider vinegar

½ tsp of sea salt, or to taste

1. In a large pot over medium-low heat, add the milk and heat until the temperature reaches 195°F (90°C), or until almost boiling. Using a wooden spoon, stir frequently to prevent the milk from scorching on the bottom of the pot.

2. As soon as the milk reaches the right temperature, remove it from the heat and stir in the vinegar.

3. Allow the milk to sit, undisturbed, for 18 to 20 minutes, or until you recognize a clean break. The milk should separate into a white solid part (curds) and a translucent liquid (whey).

4. Meanwhile, line a strainer with a double layer of cheesecloth, covering all sides. Set it on top of a large bowl for draining.

5. Gently pour the curdled milk from the pot straight into the lined strainer.

6. Let it drain in the strainer for up to 2 hours. The more time you allow it to drain, the firmer the cheese will become. I like it soft so I only let the moisture drip for about 30 minutes.

7. After the cheese has finished draining, discard the whey. Remove the cheese from the cheesecloth and transfer it to an airtight container. Season with sea salt to taste and stir to combine. Gently press the cheese into the container to bring it together and so it will take on the form of the container.

8. Store in the refrigerator until ready to use. Fresh cheese will usually last up to 7 days.

TIP: *You can flavor the cheese with the seasonings of your choice before placing it in the container. Some ideas are smoked salt flakes, minced fresh herbs or freshly cracked black pepper.*

HOMEMADE LABNEH WITH ZA'ATAR

Fresh cheeses such as labneh are tangy and extra creamy, similar to crème fraîche. The clean, fresh flavors make them the perfect vessel for your favorite flavorings. This za'atar labneh is made by straining excess liquid from full-fat yogurt, resulting in a thick, ultra-creamy spreadable cheese topped with a Middle Eastern spice blend. Notes of hearty herbs such as oregano and thyme provide intense aromas, while toasted sesame seeds add nuttiness and crunch. The refreshingly smooth and creamy cheese offsets the zesty spice blend and makes an optimal spread for bread or crackers. Labneh can also be made without the za'atar, making it an excellent replacement for any recipe that uses cream cheese or ricotta. Try the plain labneh in No-Bake Berry Cheesecake Jars (page 22). A possible side effect includes ingesting leftovers by the spoonful for a midnight snack. It's made from yogurt, so no shame is necessary, right?

TIME: About 15 minutes, plus inactive time to rest and drain | **MAKES** about 22 ounces (624 g)

MEAL: Breakfast, Snack, Appetizer

ZA'ATAR SEASONING

½ tbsp (3 g) dried oregano

1 tbsp (3 g) ground thyme

1 tbsp (7 g) sumac

1 tbsp (9 g) toasted sesame seeds

2 tsp (10 g) dried marjoram

1 tsp fine kosher salt

½ tsp freshly ground black pepper

24 oz (680 g) plain whole milk yogurt, without any additives or flavors

Extra virgin olive oil for drizzling

TIPS: *If za'atar flavor is not your cup of tea, then you can season the labneh with any herbs or spices of choice, such as freshly chopped mint, basil, parsley, smoked paprika or dried oregano.*

This homemade labneh would go well in The Classic Cheese Platter (page 142) or it can replace the feta cheese in the Strawberry and Crumbled Feta Avocado Toast (page 43).

1. To make the za'atar seasoning, in a small bowl, combine all ingredients and give it a good stir. Set aside until ready to use.

2. Line a strainer with a double layer of cheesecloth, covering all sides. Set the strainer on top of a large bowl for draining.

3. Pour the yogurt into the strainer. Bring together the sides of the cheesecloth and twist them tightly around the yogurt. Place a small plate on top of the bundle and weight it down using a heavy can or similar object.

4. Refrigerate for 12 to 24 hours. The longer you let it drain, the thicker the cheese will become. After draining, the labneh will be thick and spreadable like a soft cream cheese.

5. When the draining is complete, remove the labneh from the cheesecloth and discard the whey left in the bowl.

6. In a mixing bowl, add the labneh. Using a spatula, stir to remove the cloth markings and to make it nice and creamy. Sprinkle with the za'atar seasoning to taste. Stir well to combine.

7. Transfer the mixture to a small bowl and add a drizzle of extra virgin olive oil. The labneh can be spread on toast for breakfast, served with crackers as an appetizer or with warm pita bread on a mezze platter.

TIP: *The za'atar seasoning blend can be stored in a small, sealed container for up to 3 months. It's perfect to use not only on labneh, but for seasoning everything from vegetables to proteins, dips or soups. Feel free to adjust the seasonings to your taste.*

HOMEMADE RICOTTA CHEESE

Ricotta has a super creamy texture and mild, milky flavor, making it a fantastic cheese for using in savory and sweet applications. Homemade ricotta is even richer than the store-bought stuff and has a cleaner flavor, as it lacks preservatives. This recipe demonstrates just how easy and inexpensive it is to make ricotta at home and with just a few ingredients. Once you try this recipe for homemade whole milk ricotta, you'll never want to go back to store-bought!

PREP TIME: About 15 minutes, plus inactive time to rest and drain | **MAKES** about 12 ounces (340 g)

MEAL: Breakfast, Snack, Appetizer

½ gallon (1.9 L) whole milk

¾ tsp citric acid powder

¼ cup (60 ml) cool water

¼ cup (60 ml) heavy cream

½ tsp sea salt, or to taste

1. In a large pot over medium-low heat, add the milk and heat until the temperature reaches 195°F (90°C), or until almost boiling. Using a wooden spoon, stir frequently to prevent the milk from scorching on the bottom of the pot.

2. Meanwhile, in a small bowl, add the citric acid and cool water. Stir until fully dissolved.

3. Add the citric acid mixture to the milk. Using a wooden spoon, stir using a gentle up-and-down motion, for about 30 seconds. Almost immediately, you will see white solid parts (curds) forming. Turn off the heat and allow it to set for 45 to 60 minutes without stirring.

4. Meanwhile, line a strainer with a double layer of cheesecloth, covering all sides, leaving at least an extra 5-inch (13-cm) section of cheese-cloth hanging over. Set the strainer on top of a large bowl for draining.

5. Once the translucent liquid (whey) has settled to the bottom of the pot, use a slotted spoon to skim the curds out and into the prepared strainer.

6. Allow the cheese to drain for at least 30 minutes, or longer if you want a drier cheese.

7. Next, pull up the cheesecloth from the sides and gently twist them together to put pressure on the cheese to release more whey. The more you drain, the crumblier the cheese will get.

8. In a bowl, add the cheese and the heavy cream. Season with sea salt and stir to combine.

9. Transfer the cheese to a clean jar and refrigerate until ready to use. The cheese will stay fresh for about 5 days in the refrigerator.

TIP: *Make a double batch and use half for the Savory Cheesecake with Honey-Roasted Pears (page 130).*

HOMEMADE CREAM CHEESE WITH LEMON-HERB SEASONING

Learn how to make tangy herbed cream cheese with this simple, inexpensive recipe. From spreading on toasted bagels to dolloping on smoked salmon, this cool and creamy homemade cream cheese—full of tart lemon juice and fresh, green herbs—has many different uses. Tackling homemade cream cheese is an absolute must for any die-hard cheese fan/mad scientist hybrid.

TIME: About 15 minutes, plus inactive time to rest and drain | **MAKES** about 12 ounces (340 g)

MEAL: Breakfast, Snack, Appetizer

½ gallon (1.9 L) whole milk

¼ cup (60 ml) freshly squeezed lemon juice

2–3 tbsp (5–8 g) fresh herbs of choice, chopped

1 tsp garlic salt, or to taste

¼ tsp freshly ground black pepper

Sea salt, to taste

1. In a large pot over medium heat, add the milk and heat until almost boiling, or until the temperature reaches 195°F (90°C). Using a wooden spoon, stir frequently to prevent the milk from scorching on the bottom of the pot.

2. As soon as the milk reaches the right temperature, remove it from the heat and stir in the lemon juice.

3. Allow the milk to sit, undisturbed, for 15 minutes, or until the white solid parts (curds) float to the top and separate from the translucent liquid (whey).

4. Meanwhile, line a strainer with a double layer of cheesecloth, covering all sides. Set it on top of a large bowl for draining.

5. Gently pour all the contents from the pot into the lined colander and allow the curds to drain for about 45 minutes.

6. Transfer the drained curds to a food processor and add the herbs, garlic salt and pepper. Pulse until it forms a soft, creamy cheese ball. Taste and add salt, as needed.

7. Place the cream cheese in an airtight container. Refrigerate for at least 1 hour before eating to allow the flavors to fully develop. The cheese will stay fresh up to 1 week in the refrigerator.

BRIE, FETA & GOAT CHEESE

Flavor-Packed Dishes with Lush and Creamy Soft Cheeses

Soft cheeses, including Brie, feta and goat cheese, have a creamy texture and delicate, balanced flavor. Biting into a soft cheese is a dream-like experience as the cheese slightly melts in your mouth and coats your tongue. These cheeses should be treated and stored with care so that they can retain their usability for as long as possible. With thinner, softer rinds than harder cheeses, soft cheese should always be wrapped in wax paper to keep it from drying out and to prevent outside odors and bacteria from getting in.

There is nothing else like Brie, with its signature soft rind and rich, creamy interior. At room temperature, Brie seems unassuming. The edible rind is somewhat flavorless and the inside is slightly sticky to the touch, with a beautiful buttery, mellow flavor. When melted, however, Brie gets ooey-gooey and its buttery flavor intensifies. Try simply baking a wheel of Brie and dipping vegetables into the soft, gooey interior, or slice it and let it melt over potatoes (see page 48).

Feta is an extremely popular cheese with a signature salty, briny flavor. Feta has a pleasantly dry texture, reminiscent of cheese curds. It has a similar flavor to halloumi, but with more salinity and a crumblier texture. Use feta to give any dish a pop of flavor and an extra bit of salt. It also makes a flavorful garnish for sprinkling on the Greek Avocado Toast (page 63) or tacos.

Goat cheese is gaining steam and being used more and more to lend a creamy texture and tangy flavor to salads, soups and many other dishes. It's a great cheese to use when you are looking for something that isn't too salty but still provides wonderful richness and creaminess.

In this chapter, you'll learn how to use different soft-textured cheeses and which flavors go best with them. Whether you melt, crumble or fry them, soft cheeses are always delicious and deserve some TLC.

While Brie, feta and goat cheese are some of the most popular soft cheeses, there are many more varieties and substitutions on the market. Boursin cheese is a wonderful, garlicky herb-flavored cheese that looks a lot like goat cheese but doesn't have its signature tang. It makes a wonderful spread for bread or crackers and can be melted into mac and cheese. Stracchino is another popular cheese that is soft, mild and spreadable. It can be used as a pizza topping, or as a replacement for Brie. Camembert is another soft cheese with a bloomy rind that is often confused with Brie. Brie has a higher milk fat content, making it a little richer than Camembert, but Camembert is a fine substitution.

SESAME-CRUSTED FETA WITH CRUNCHY SAUTÉED VEGGIES

Salty feta cheese is extremely versatile, making itself at home when crumbled on salads, stirred into cream sauces or coated in batter and lightly fried. This Sesame-Crusted Feta with Crunchy Sautéed Veggies presents large pieces of feta that have been fully coated in sesame seeds. After being pan-fried, the sesame seeds become nice and toasted, while the feta warms and becomes fragrant. The feta is amazing on its own but also makes the perfect topper for crisp sautéed pepper, red onion, zucchini and asparagus. With a colorful base of fresh vegetables and a topping of the craveable fried cheese, this is a healthy vegetarian main course that any cheese lover will adore. The salty feta and crisp vegetables pair well with dry white wines, such as Sauvignon Blanc or Chenin Blanc.

PREP TIME: 15 minutes | **COOK TIME:** about 25 minutes | **MAKES** 4 servings
MEAL: Lunch, Dinner

SESAME-CRUSTED FETA

¼ cup (31 g) flour, gluten free if needed

2 large eggs, beaten

⅓ cup (48 g) sesame seeds

16 oz (454 g) feta cheese, blocks cut in half diagonally

2 tbsp (30 ml) avocado or olive oil

SAUTÉED VEGGIES

1 tbsp (15 ml) avocado or olive oil

2 large bell peppers, cut into matchsticks

1 medium red onion, sliced

1 medium zucchini, cut into half moons

¼ lb (113 g) asparagus, ends trimmed and halved

1–2 large cloves garlic, minced

2–3 fresh oregano stems

½ lemon, zested and juiced

Sea salt and freshly ground black pepper, to taste

Oregano leaves, for garnishing

1. To make the sesame-crusted feta, set out three shallow dishes or bowls and add the flour to one, the beaten eggs to another and the sesame seeds to the last.

2. Coat each piece of the feta cheese with the flour, shaking off any excess so there is only a very thin layer of flour on it. Add the feta to the beaten eggs and coat evenly on all sides. Make sure not to leave any dry patches so the sesame seeds will stick.

3. Finally, coat the cheese with the sesame seeds, gently pressing so the seeds adhere and evenly coat the feta on all sides.

4. In a nonstick pan over medium-low heat, heat the oil. Once hot, carefully add the sesame-coated feta and fry until the crust is golden and crispy, for 3 to 4 minutes on each side. Use tongs to gently flip the fried feta and cook it evenly on all sides.

5. Once cooked, place the feta on a paper towel to absorb any excess oil. You might need to work in two batches to cook the feta, as it's very important not to overcrowd the pan.

6. To make the veggies, wipe the pan clean and pour in the oil. Heat over medium-high heat and, once the oil is shimmering, add the bell peppers, onion, zucchini and asparagus. Sauté for 3 to 4 minutes. Add the garlic, oregano, lemon zest, lemon juice, salt and pepper. Continue to stir and cook for 2 to 3 minutes longer, frequently tossing the veggies with a wooden spatula. The veggies should have a crunch to the bite, so be careful not to overcook them.

7. Transfer the veggies to a platter and top with the sesame-crusted feta. Garnish with the fresh oregano leaves.

STRAWBERRY AND CRUMBLED FETA AVOCADO TOAST

Salty feta and sweet, fresh strawberries are a fun way to add pops of color and flavor to everyday avocado toast. Steeping the strawberries in syrupy balsamic vinegar brings out their flavorful juices and adds a beautiful tang to the whole situation. A sprinkling of briny Greek feta adds a uniquely salty bite that you just don't get from plain salt. Finish the avocado toast with a handful of sprouts and a spoonful of the syrupy vinegar for a breakfast or lunch to enjoy any day of the week. With the perfect balance of sweet and salty elements, this unique take on avocado toast is a great way to enjoy a light breakfast when under a time crunch without sacrificing flavor.

PREP TIME: 10 minutes | **MAKES** 4 servings

MEAL: Breakfast, Lunch

2 cups (332 g) ripe strawberries, chopped

2 tbsp (30 ml) good-quality balsamic vinegar

1 large ripe avocado, or 2 small ones

1 tbsp (15 ml) lemon juice, freshly squeezed

Sea salt and freshly ground black pepper, to taste

4 slices of crusty toasted bread

8 oz (226 g) feta or goat cheese, crumbled

Small handful of sprouts, to sprinkle

1. In a mixing bowl, add the chopped strawberries and drizzle with the balsamic vinegar. Toss well and let it sit at room temperature for about 5 minutes to meld the flavors.

2. Meanwhile, slice the avocado in half and, using a spoon, scoop the flesh out into a bowl. Squeeze the fresh lemon juice over the avocado and season with a pinch of salt and pepper. Mash with a fork to your desired texture.

3. Top the toasted bread slices with a layer of mashed avocado.

4. Divide the feta cheese and balsamic strawberries among the 4 toast slices. Sprinkle with a handful of sprouts and freshly ground black pepper, to taste.

5. Drizzle with any remaining balsamic vinegar from the bowl of strawberries.

TIPS: *Avocado toast is such a nourishing breakfast that's also very quick to put together in the morning. The night before, prepare small individual containers with the crumbled feta, chopped strawberries and mashed avocado with a touch of lemon juice and refrigerate. This way, you'll only need to toast the bread, add the toppings and dig in! Oh, what a great way to start your day!*

Use an aged Balsamic of Modena vinegar, which is denser, sweeter and more flavorful than regular balsamic. It has a lower acidity and a more balanced sweet-and-sour taste.

HERB-MARINATED GOAT CHEESE

Herb-encrusted goat cheese makes for a super simple yet elegant appetizer.
Tangy fresh cheese combined with a mixture of fresh chives, dill and oregano is simply
divine when served alongside crackers or bread. Not only does this easy dish taste amazing,
it serves as a festive table centerpiece for holidays. Tangy goat cheese and herbs pair
extremely well with grassy Sauvignon Blanc or Sancerre.

PREP TIME: 15 minutes | **MAKES** 8 servings

MEAL: Breakfast, Appetizer

12 oz (340 g) log of goat cheese

2 cloves garlic, thinly sliced

Small bunch of fresh chives

Small handful of fresh dill

Small handful of fresh oregano leaves

Small handful of fresh parsley leaves

1 cup (240 ml) extra virgin olive oil,
or enough to cover the cheese

Salt flakes and freshly ground black
pepper, to taste

1. Using a very sharp knife, slice the goat cheese log into ¼-inch (6-mm)-thick rounds. The goat cheese is very delicate, so be gentle when slicing it so that the rounds keep their shape.

2. Place the cheese rounds in a wide, glass container, preferably with a lid.

3. Place the garlic slices on top of the cheese and sprinkle with the chives, dill, oregano and parsley.

4. Pour in the oil and sprinkle with the salt flakes and freshly ground pepper. There should be enough oil to cover all of the goat cheese slices.

5. Cover the container and keep refrigerated until ready to serve or up to 7 days. Serve the cheese with crusty bread, fresh veggies or in your favorite salad. The oil makes a delicious dressing for salads when combined with a splash of good-quality balsamic vinegar.

TIP: *To easily slice the goat cheese, you can use dental floss; just make sure it is not a flavored type.*

GOAT CHEESE BERRY SALAD

Tart, creamy goat cheese makes the perfect pairing for late summer berries,
contrasting rich cheese and refreshingly juicy pops of fruit. In this lovely green spinach salad,
a trio of summer berries are paired with sweet, crisp corn kernels, a slightly sweet citrus
vinaigrette and gobs of tangy goat cheese for richness. This salad is the best friend of any meat
dish but also makes a great accompaniment for picnics, especially if you pack
some extra goat cheese and berries for snacking.

PREP TIME: 10 minutes | **MAKES** 4–6 servings

MEAL: Lunch, Appetizer

DRESSING

¼ cup (60 ml) extra virgin olive oil

3 tbsp (45 ml) freshly squeezed lemon juice

1 tsp lime zest

1 tbsp (15 ml) honey

Sea salt and freshly ground black pepper, to taste

SALAD

5 oz (142 g) baby spinach, washed and dried

1 English cucumber, thinly sliced

1 small red onion, thinly sliced

1 (15-oz [425-g]) can corn, drained

14 oz (397 g) goat cheese crumbles

8 oz (226 g) fresh strawberries, sliced

6 oz (170 g) fresh raspberries, washed and pat-dried

4 oz (113 g) fresh blueberries, washed and pat-dried

1. To make the dressing, in a small bowl, whisk all the dressing ingredients until emulsified.

2. In a large bowl, add the baby spinach, cucumber, onion and corn. Pour the dressing over and toss until evenly coated.

3. Top with the goat cheese crumbles and fresh berries. Give it a good toss before serving.

TIP: *You can also use 4 to 5 ears of fresh corn on the cob. Cut the kernels off each ear and then sauté or quickly boil the kernels. Drain and cool.*

BRIE ROSEMARY POTATO BAKE

Rich, buttery Brie makes the perfect companion to herby rosemary potatoes. Thinly slicing potatoes on a mandoline ensures that each piece of potato cooks until it's perfectly tender. Tangy sour cream helps form a rich sauce that coats the potatoes while the fresh garlic and herbs infuse the potatoes with a delicate aroma and flavor. The slices of Brie, melted over the potato bake, turn the rich and creamy cheesy potatoes into a magical experience. Brie pairs beautifully with rich, acidic white wines, such as Chardonnay, or light-bodied reds, such as Pinot Noir.

PREP TIME: 15 minutes | **COOK TIME:** 47 minutes | **MAKES** 4 dinner servings or 6–8 side dish servings

MEAL: Dinner, Side Dish

6 medium Yukon gold potatoes (about 2 lbs [900 g]), peeled

3 cloves garlic, minced or pressed

4 tbsp (57 g) salted butter, melted, divided, plus more to grease the pan

6 fresh thyme sprigs, leaves picked

2 large fresh rosemary sprigs, leaves picked and chopped

Salt flakes and freshly ground black pepper, to taste

1½ cups (360 ml) sour cream

8 oz (226 g) Brie, sliced

1. Preheat the oven to 350°F (180°C).

2. Thinly slice the potatoes with a mandoline or a very sharp knife. Place the potato slices in a large bowl.

3. Add the garlic, 3 tablespoons (43 g) of the melted butter, thyme and rosemary. Season with salt flakes and pepper. Using your hands, gently toss to combine and evenly coat the slices.

4. Grease an oven-safe skillet or a round baking dish with a bit of butter.

5. Add a ½-inch (1.3-cm) layer of sliced potatoes to the skillet. Spread ½ cup (120 ml) of the sour cream over the potatoes. Top with a few slices of Brie. Repeat until all the ingredients are nicely layered in the skillet. You should have 3 layers of potatoes. Reserve a few Brie slices to use as a topping decoration.

6. Brush the top with the remaining 1 tablespoon (14 g) of the melted butter. Cover with aluminum foil and place on the middle rack of the oven.

7. Bake for about 45 minutes, or until bubbly and the potatoes are tender when pierced with a fork.

8. Remove from the oven and arrange the remaining Brie slices on top of the potatoes.

9. Turn on the broiler and return the skillet to the oven. Broil for 2 to 3 minutes, or until golden-brown on top.

TIP: *The easiest and quickest way to slice the potatoes thinly is to use a mandoline. Be very careful though, as this tool can quickly hurt you. To slice the potatoes while keeping your fingers intact, set the mandoline on a clean wooden chopping board and make sure it doesn't have any movement. Set the thickness to the thinnest setting. Place one potato at a time inside the hand guard, then slide it onto the blade to get nice even slices. Never use a mandoline without a hand guard as it can easily slice off the tip of your finger.*

CHICKEN PEACH QUINOA BOWLS WITH CRUMBLED FETA

In this refreshing summer chicken salad, dry and crumbly feta is paired with intensely sweet grilled peaches for a salty-sweet flavor combo that will please any craving. Steamed quinoa is the perfect base for letting these flavors and textures shine. A lightly sweetened lemon vinaigrette brings all the flavors to life and highlights the fresh feta's tanginess.

PREP TIME: 15 minutes | **COOK TIME:** 40 minutes | **MAKES** 4 servings

MEAL: Lunch or Dinner

LEMONY VINAIGRETTE

3 tbsp (45 ml) fresh lemon juice

1 tsp lemon zest (from 1 lemon)

1 tbsp (15 ml) apple cider vinegar

1–2 cloves garlic, minced

1 tbsp (15 ml) maple syrup

¼ cup (60 ml) extra virgin olive oil

Pinch of red pepper flakes

¾ tsp sea salt

¼ tsp freshly ground black pepper

SALAD

10 oz (283 g) mixed cherry tomatoes, halved

¾ cup (135 g) Kalamata olives, pitted

¾ tsp sea salt, or to taste

¼ tsp freshly ground pepper, or to taste

1 cup (170 g) quinoa, rinsed

1¾ cups (420 ml) water or vegetable broth

1 tsp garlic powder

1 tsp onion powder

1½ tsp (4.5 g) dried oregano

1½ lbs (680 g) chicken breasts

1 tbsp (15 ml) extra virgin olive oil

2 large peaches, halved and pitted

10 oz (283 g) feta cheese, crumbled

Broccoli sprouts (optional)

1. To make the vinaigrette, in a small mixing bowl, add all of the ingredients and whisk until combined. Adjust the seasonings to taste. In a large mixing bowl, add the tomatoes, olives and the prepared vinaigrette. Season with salt and pepper if needed. Toss well and set aside.

2. In a medium saucepan over medium-low heat, add the quinoa and water. Cover and bring to a boil. Reduce the heat to low and simmer for about 15 minutes, or until cooked through. When the quinoa has finished cooking, remove it from the heat and let it sit, covered, for about 10 minutes. Fluff with a fork and allow it to cool.

3. Meanwhile, in a small bowl, mix the garlic powder, onion powder, oregano, sea salt and pepper. Sprinkle the chicken with this seasoning mix and drizzle a spoonful of the olive oil on top. Rub the chicken breasts on all sides to nicely coat them. If time allows, marinate, covered, for 1 to 3 hours in the refrigerator.

4. Brush the grill with a bit of oil and heat over medium-high heat. Grill the chicken until each side is nicely charred and the chicken is cooked through, 6 to 10 minutes per side depending on the thickness of the breasts. Once the chicken is done, remove from the heat and set aside to rest. When cool enough to touch, shred or slice into bite-size pieces.

5. Next, place the peaches, cut side down, on the heated grill. Cook undisturbed until grill marks appear, for 6 to 8 minutes. Remove and cut into thin slices.

6. To assemble the salad, add the quinoa to a large serving bowl. Spoon out the tomato and olives from the vinaigrette and place on top of the quinoa. Add the feta cheese. Pour the juices from the tomato-olive mixture over the salad. Add the shredded chicken and grilled peaches. Garnish with the broccoli sprouts (if using) and toss to combine.

FETA-LOADED PANZANELLA SALAD

Large cubes of feta cheese make this bread salad perfect for any cheese lover. Begin with a base of toasted ciabatta bread cubes and toss with juicy chopped tomatoes, sliced cucumber, sweet red bell pepper, briny oil-cured olives, sharp red onion and a hefty portion of cubed feta cheese. A tart lemon dressing, infused with lots of herbs, tames the assertively salty feta and makes it the shining star in this cheesy take on the classy panzanella salad. Don't be surprised if you find yourself licking your plate!

PREP TIME: 20 minutes | **COOK TIME:** 10 minutes | **MAKES** 6 servings

MEAL: Lunch, Dinner, Appetizer

DRESSING

2 tbsp (30 ml) white wine vinegar

2 tbsp (30 ml) lemon juice, freshly squeezed

¼ cup (60 ml) extra virgin olive oil

1 clove garlic, minced

½ tsp dried oregano

½ tsp dried basil

½ tsp kosher salt

¼ tsp freshly ground black pepper

SALAD

1 large loaf ciabatta or French bread

2 tbsp (30 ml) olive oil

Kosher salt and freshly ground black pepper, to taste

10 oz (283 g) tomatoes of choice, chopped into bite-size pieces

1 English cucumber, thinly sliced

1 large red bell pepper, chopped

1 cup (180 g) oil-cured black olives

1 small red onion, thinly sliced

8 oz (226 g) feta cheese, cubed

1. Preheat the oven to 375°F (190°C). Line a large, rimmed sheet pan with parchment paper.

2. To make the dressing, in a small jar, add all the dressing ingredients. Screw the lid on tightly and shake vigorously to emulsify.

3. Using a sharp bread knife, carefully cut the ciabatta into 1-inch (2.5-cm) cubes.

4. Place the bread cubes on the prepared sheet pan. Drizzle with the olive oil and sprinkle with a pinch of salt and pepper.

5. Bake in the oven for about 10 minutes, or until the bread is nicely toasted. Remove from the oven and allow it to cool. It will get crispier as it cools.

6. Meanwhile, in a large bowl, mix the tomatoes, cucumber, bell pepper, olives, red onion and feta cheese. Add the dressing and toss until well combined.

7. Once the toasted bread is cooled, add it to the salad bowl and give the salad another good toss.

8. Let the salad sit for 15 to 20 minutes to meld the flavors and allow the bread to soak up all the delicious tomato juices.

TIP: *This filling, Italian-inspired bread salad works great as a light main entree, especially for potlucks or when you need a portable meal for work lunches. Make it ahead and take it with you to go.*

FETA QUINOA TABBOULEH

Feta cheese is the perfect addition to grain salads, such as this unique tabbouleh. A base of steamed, protein-packed quinoa is tossed with sweet pomegranate arils, juicy cherry tomatoes, diced cucumber, fresh parsley and mint, scallions, crunchy sunflower seeds, lots of deliciously briny feta and a garlicky lemon vinaigrette. Thanks to the flavorful punch of cheesy feta, this healthy tabbouleh salad gives any meal the cheesy side dish it was missing.

PREP TIME: 25 minutes | **MAKES** 8 servings

MEAL: Lunch, Side Dish

DRESSING

¼ cup (60 ml) extra virgin olive oil

1 large lemon, zested and juiced

2–3 cloves garlic, minced

¾ tsp sea salt, or to taste

¼ tsp freshly ground black pepper, or to taste

TABBOULEH

1½ cups (255 g) quinoa

3 cups (720 ml) water or vegetable broth

Sea salt and freshly ground black pepper, to taste

10 oz (283 g) barrel-aged feta cheese, crumbled

1 large pomegranate, seeded

14 oz (397 g) cherry or grape tomatoes, cut into quarters

1 English (or 2 Persian) cucumber, diced

1 large bunch of fresh parsley, finely chopped

1 small bunch of fresh mint, finely chopped

¼ cup (12 g) green onions or scallions, thinly sliced

½ cup (67 g) sunflower seeds

1. To make the dressing, in a small bowl, add all the dressing ingredients and whisk to emulsify. Set aside.

2. Rinse the quinoa through a fine mesh strainer until the water runs clear.

3. In a medium saucepan over medium heat, add the quinoa and water. Season with salt and pepper. Bring to a boil, cover and reduce the heat to medium-low. Simmer until tender, for about 15 minutes. You'll know it's done when you start seeing the little "tails" of quinoa popping out.

4. Remove the quinoa from the heat and drain any excess water. Place in a large bowl and set aside to cool.

5. Meanwhile, prepare the vegetables. When the quinoa is cooled, add the feta cheese, pomegranate seeds, tomatoes, cucumber, parsley, mint, green onions and sunflower seeds.

6. Pour the dressing over the mixture and gently toss to incorporate. Add salt and pepper to taste.

SAVORY PANCAKES WITH CRUMBLED FETA AND CHIVES

Feta cheese and oniony chives are a flavor combination that works extremely well in savory pancakes. These gluten-free pancakes are made with oat flour and lots of flavorful seasonings. They are loaded with chunks of feta and chopped chives that are folded directly into the batter. Cooking them in bacon fat gives them a crisp, smoky crust, while the inside remains light and fluffy. Top the pancakes with your favorite toppings, such as more crumbled feta, crispy bacon and sliced avocado. Don't be afraid to pour on maple syrup; its sweetness will mellow out all of the salty flavors going on. Dig into these cheesy goodies while they're hot.

PREP TIME: 5–10 minutes | **COOK TIME:** 15–25 minutes | **MAKES** 4–6 servings

MEAL: Breakfast, Lunch, Appetizer

2¼ cups (205 g) old-fashioned rolled oats

2 tsp (9 g) baking powder

½ tsp sea salt, or to taste

¼ tsp freshly ground black pepper, or to taste

2 large eggs

1 cup (240 ml) milk

1 tsp onion powder

½ tsp garlic powder

½ tsp chili powder, or to taste

6 oz (170 g) feta cheese, crumbled

3 tbsp (9 g) chives, thinly sliced

8 slices of bacon

OPTIONAL TOPPINGS

Avocado slices, crumbled cheese, maple syrup

1. Place the oats, baking powder, salt and pepper in a blender or food processor and pulse until the mixture resembles flour.

2. Add the eggs, milk, onion powder, garlic powder and chili powder. Blend until smooth, about 45 seconds. Season with a pinch of salt and pepper. Using a spatula, gently fold in the feta cheese and chives. Set aside.

3. In a large nonstick pan over medium heat, cook the bacon until crispy or to your liking. Remove the bacon, reserving the fat in the pan for now, and set aside on a paper towel to cool.

4. In a small bowl, transfer the fat from the pan and use it to cook the pancakes. You'll need to grease the pan lightly with a pastry brush before adding each pancake.

5. In the greased, hot pan, add about ⅓ cup (80 ml) of the batter. Cook over medium heat for 2 to 3 minutes or until bubbles appear on the surface. Gently flip the pancake over and cook for 1 to 2 minutes longer. Remove from the pan and set aside on a plate.

6. Repeat with the remaining batter, lightly greasing the pan with the bacon fat between each pancake. Cover the cooked pancakes as you go to keep them warm.

7. Divide the pancakes and stack them on individual plates. Add the bacon and your toppings of choice.

TIP: *To add more texture to this dish, fold some bigger pieces of feta into the pancake batter.*

ROASTED SWEET POTATO SALAD WITH BACON AND GOAT CHEESE

Creamy goat cheese is the perfect way to tame the robust flavors in this hearty sweet potato and lettuce salad. Chunks of sweet potatoes are roasted with a mixture of olive oil, maple syrup and seasonings, giving them an intensely sweet, caramelized exterior. Crispy bacon balances the sweetness with smoky, salty flavors. A sweet maple vinaigrette rounds out all the flavors. Vibrantly tangy goat cheese brings brightness to heartier fall salads like this one. The smoky bacon and goat cheese pair wonderfully with a crisp Rosé.

PREP TIME: 15 minutes | **COOK TIME:** 18–20 minutes | **MAKES** 4 servings

MEAL: Lunch, Appetizer

1 lb (454 g) sweet potatoes, scrubbed and unpeeled

1 tbsp (15 ml) avocado or olive oil

1 tbsp (15 ml) maple syrup

1 tsp garlic salt, or to taste

Sea salt and freshly ground black pepper, to taste

4 oz (113 g) bacon slices, thinly cut

5 oz (142 g) mixed leafy greens

1 pomegranate, seeded

8 oz (226 g) goat cheese, sliced

1 tbsp (4 g) fresh parsley, chopped, for garnishing

MAPLE DRESSING

2 tbsp (30 ml) apple cider vinegar

¼ cup (60 ml) extra virgin olive oil

1 tbsp (15 ml) maple syrup

1 tsp Dijon mustard

Sea salt and freshly ground black pepper, to taste

TIP: *You can easily double this recipe for a main meal.*

1. Preheat the oven to 400°F (200°C). Line two sheet pans with parchment paper.

2. Cut the sweet potatoes in half lengthwise and then slice into ¼-inch (0.6-cm) half-moons.

3. In a large bowl, add the sweet potatoes and drizzle with the oil and maple syrup. Season to taste with the garlic salt, sea salt and pepper.

4. Toss well to get all pieces nicely coated. Layer them evenly on one of the prepared sheet pans.

5. On the second sheet pan, arrange the bacon slices, leaving a bit of space in between to cook and crisp them evenly.

6. Place both trays in the preheated oven and bake for 18 to 20 minutes, or until the bacon is crispy and the sweet potatoes are tender and slightly caramelized. Keep an eye on them as they roast, turning the potatoes after about 10 minutes.

7. Meanwhile, to make the maple dressing, in a small jar, add all the dressing ingredients. Screw the lid on tightly and shake vigorously to emulsify.

8. Once the bacon and sweet potatoes are done, remove them from the oven and allow to cool for a few minutes.

9. In a large bowl, add the mixed greens and pomegranate seeds. Pour in the dressing. Gently toss to combine and coat the greens.

10. Top with the roasted sweet potatoes, goat cheese and crispy bacon. Garnish with the parsley.

FETA PEACH SUMMER SALAD

Salty, tangy feta cheese is a classic pairing for juicy, sweet summer fruits such as peaches. One of the saltiest cheeses, feta shines when crumbled and used as a finishing touch to a soup or salad. Here, sliced peaches, juicy cherry tomatoes, cool cucumber and sweet red onion are lightly tossed with olive oil, balsamic vinegar, sprouts and crumbled feta. A short marinade in the vinaigrette brings out all of the fresh juices, making this a refreshingly light salad for the hottest summer days. Thanks to the crumbly feta, the syrupy juices in this salad are balanced with a pop of briny saltiness. Summer salads with fruit and fresh cheese can be served with sweet white wines, such as Riesling, or any sparkling wine.

PREP TIME: 15 minutes | **MAKES** 4 servings

MEAL: Lunch, Appetizer

2 large ripe peaches

10 oz (283 g) cherry or grape tomatoes

1 English cucumber, sliced

4 radishes, sliced into matchsticks, or chopped

1 small red onion, peeled and halved

7 oz (198 g) feta cheese, crumbled

Handful of sprouts of choice, such as red cabbage sprouts

2–3 tbsp (30–45 ml) good-quality balsamic vinegar

2 tbsp (30 ml) extra virgin olive oil

Sea salt and freshly ground black pepper, to taste

1. Use a very sharp chef's knife and a clean chopping board to prepare the fresh ingredients. Place the peaches on your chopping board and, starting at the stem, cut them in half. With your hands, gently twist each side of the peach in opposite directions to pull them apart into halves. Remove the pits, then place the peach, cut side down, on the chopping board and slice it.

2. Next, cut the tomatoes in half. Thinly slice the cucumber, radishes and onion.

3. In a large bowl, add the peaches, tomatoes, cucumber, radishes and onion. Sprinkle with the crumbled feta cheese and sprouts.

4. Drizzle with the balsamic vinegar and olive oil. Season to taste with salt and pepper.

5. Toss well to combine. Allow the salad to sit for about 5 minutes so the juices can meld.

GREEK AVOCADO TOAST

A double dose of feta turns ordinary avocado toast from boring to something you'll crave for breakfast on a daily basis. The real flavor in this Greek avocado toast starts by spreading toasted sourdough with mashed avocado that's been mixed with briny feta cheese, minced garlic, tangy lemon juice and oregano. Top the whole shebang with diced cucumber, sweet cherry tomatoes, salty, chopped olives and more of the deliciously addictive feta. A drizzle of olive oil is the last step before enjoying a breakfast that you can feel good about eating in more ways than one.

PREP TIME: 10–15 minutes | **MAKES** 4 servings

MEAL: Breakfast, Lunch, Snack

2 ripe avocados, pits removed

8 oz (226 g) feta cheese, crumbled, divided

1 small clove garlic, minced

2 tbsp (30 ml) freshly squeezed lemon juice

1 tsp dried oregano

Kosher salt and freshly ground black pepper, to taste

4 slices sourdough bread, toasted

¼ English cucumber, diced

5 oz (142 g) cherry tomatoes, halved

½ small red onion, diced

¾ cup (135 g) black olives, pitted and halved

Extra virgin olive oil, for drizzling

1. In a medium bowl, add the flesh from the avocados and mash with a fork until chunky.

2. Add 4 ounces (113 g) of the feta cheese, garlic, lemon juice, oregano, salt and pepper and mash thoroughly until well combined.

3. Divide the avocado mixture between the 4 sourdough slices and spread it evenly with a fork.

4. Top with the diced cucumber, cherry tomatoes, onion and olives. Sprinkle with the remaining 4 ounces (113 g) of the feta cheese. Drizzle with olive oil and serve.

MEDITERRANEAN TRAY BAKE

This Mediterranean tray bake is a hearty one-pan vegetarian supper loaded with strong flavors, thanks to generous chunks of feta cheese and roasted veggies. Sweet tomatoes, a whole head of garlic and olives are roasted until juicy and caramelized, along with sourdough bread cubes that get nice and crispy. Top the simple tray bake with fresh basil for a light summer meal that will bring loads of flavor to the party.

PREP TIME: 10 minutes | **COOK TIME:** 40 minutes | **MAKES** 4 servings

MEAL: Lunch, Dinner

1 whole garlic head

9 oz (255 g) feta cheese, cut into large cubes

1 lb (454 g) mixed tomatoes, leave the small ones whole and cut the large ones in half

½ cup (90 g) mixed olives, pitted

4 slices of ½-inch (1.3-cm)-thick sourdough bread, torn into chunks

Sea salt and freshly ground black pepper, to taste

2 tbsp (30 ml) extra virgin olive oil

Small bunch of fresh basil, for garnishing

1. Preheat the oven to 320°F (160°C).

2. Peel away the loose outer layers around the garlic head. Make sure you leave the head intact with all cloves connected. Then cut the garlic head in half, horizontally, to expose the cloves.

3. In a baking dish or a rimmed sheet pan, add the garlic, feta cheese, tomatoes, olives and sourdough chunks. Season to taste with salt and pepper and drizzle with the olive oil.

4. Place the dish on the middle rack of the preheated oven. Bake for 30 to 40 minutes, or until the tomatoes are slightly charred and the feta is golden-brown on the sides.

5. Once roasted, remove from the oven and allow to cool for about 10 minutes. Remove the garlic skin and garnish with the fresh basil leaves.

TIP: *Dip the toasted, crusty bread into the soft, buttery feta cheese and then mop up all the tomato juices left in the tray.*

STILTON, ROQUEFORT & GORGONZOLA

Meals with Pungent, Rich and Smooth Semi-Soft Cheeses

Blue-veined cheeses are unmarked territory for many people. The minute they hear about cheese containing mold, picky eaters scurry away like an army of ants. What they don't understand is that not all mold is created equal. Cultures of Penicillium are intentionally incorporated into the wheels of blue cheese and are entirely edible. While you wouldn't enjoy eating those cultures alone, when combined with the tangy flavors of lactic acid and the generous amount of salt in the cheese, the pungent flavor becomes a positive aspect.

Blue-veined cheeses are so under-appreciated, it's honestly a travesty. They have a strong flavor, but where people go wrong is how they use blue cheeses. As with all cheeses, blue-veined cheese comes in a variety of types and each type shines in different applications. For example, on the milder side of things is English Stilton. While one of the easiest blue cheeses to eat for newbies, it's also one of the most complex. It's rich and creamy but also sweet, salty and nutty. This makes it very versatile, whether crumbled into an Apple and Stilton Salad with Roasted Hazelnuts (page 80) or folded into rich and creamy Bacon and Stilton Mashed Potatoes (page 83).

On the stronger side of things is Italian Gorgonzola. It comes in two varieties: Gorgonzola Dolce and Gorgonzola Piccante. The dolce variety is creamier and slightly sweet, while the piccante type has a crumbly texture and spicy flavor. The two varieties can be used interchangeably but will slightly affect the flavor of a recipe, depending on which type is used. Gorgonzola tastes delicious melted into cream sauces—try my Blue Mac & Cheese (page 75) with Gorgonzola—or crumbled into a Roasted Red Pepper and Tomato Soup with Gorgonzola Piccante (page 68). Gorgonzola is a great cheese to use when you want to give a dish some extra salt and a kick of flavor.

Finally, there is French Roquefort cheese. One of the most divisive blue cheeses, it's considered the king for those who enjoy something sharper than everyday cheese. With an intense aroma and piquant, pungent flavor, those who have learned how to use it know that it's all about using other ingredients to balance Roquefort's stronger flavor. Sweet, caramelized squash sweetens up some of Gorgonzola's strong, savory flavors in my Twice-Baked Butternut Squash with Gorgonzola (page 72), while the intensity of Roquefort mellows with the help of rich cream, in my Creamy Roquefort Chicken Gnocchi (page 79).

In this chapter, you'll learn that blue cheese isn't just for crumbling onto a salad. When used correctly, it can be incorporated into almost any dish without overwhelming the other flavors. Whether you want a mild Stilton, or an intensely rich Roquefort, blue cheese always has a place on the table.

ROASTED RED PEPPER AND TOMATO SOUP WITH GORGONZOLA PICCANTE

Piccante, or *piquant*, is a term used to denote spiciness. The spice in the cheese is not overpowering but becomes more present because Gorgonzola Piccante is less sweet than the other variety, Gorgonzola Dolce. In this zesty soup, where red bell peppers become extra sweet when roasted and combined with the juicy vine-ripened tomatoes and smoky paprika, a punch of salty cheese is welcomed with open arms. This gourmet take on tomato soup mellows the strong flavors of the Gorgonzola Piccante while allowing it to remain front and center. Serve the soup with a dry, crisp white wine, such as an Albarino or Pinot Grigio.

PREP TIME: 15–20 minutes | **COOK TIME:** 40 minutes | **MAKES** 4 servings

MEAL: Lunch, Appetizer, Dinner

4 red bell peppers, halved and seeded

18 oz (510 g) fresh vine tomatoes, halved

2 tbsp (30 ml) olive oil

Sea salt and freshly ground black pepper, to taste

1½ tsp (4 g) smoked paprika

2 tbsp (28 g) salted butter

1 sweet onion, peeled and diced

2 ribs celery, thinly sliced

2–3 cloves garlic, chopped

1 tbsp (16 g) tomato paste

2 cups (480 ml) vegetable broth

5½ oz (156 g) Gorgonzola Piccante, crumbled and divided

Crusty baguette or garlic bread, for serving (optional)

1. Preheat the oven to 400°F (200°C). Line a large rimmed sheet pan with parchment paper.

2. Place the prepared peppers and tomato halves, cut side down, onto the sheet pan. Drizzle with the olive oil and sprinkle with the salt, pepper and smoked paprika. Using clean hands, gently toss in the pan to nicely coat in the oil and spices. Place the pan on the upper rack of your preheated oven and bake for 25 to 30 minutes, or until the vegetables are tender and lightly charred.

3. Meanwhile, in a large pot or Dutch oven over medium heat, melt the butter. Add the onion, celery and garlic and sauté for 4 to 5 minutes. Stir in the tomato paste and vegetable broth and remove from the heat.

4. Once the roasted veggies are done, remove the sheet pan from the oven and let it cool until ready to handle. Carefully remove and discard the skin from the peppers and tomatoes. Add the veggies to the pot with the broth, along with all the juices from the pan, and return the pot to medium heat. Bring the soup to a boil and then reduce the heat and simmer for about 10 minutes to allow all the flavors to meld.

5. Turn off the heat and stir in 2 ounces (57 g) of the Gorgonzola Piccante. Using a hand blender, carefully blend the soup until smooth. Alternatively, transfer the soup to a blender (blend in batches, if needed) and blend until smooth.

6. Ladle the soup into bowls and top with the remaining 3½ ounces (99 g) of the Gorgonzola Piccante. Sprinkle with freshly ground black pepper. Serve with the crusty baguette or garlic bread, if using.

BLUE CHEESE, CRANBERRY AND SPINACH PASTA

Blue cheese lovers and skeptics alike will love this approachable pasta. Sweetening it with fruits, such as dried cranberries, balances its strong flavors and allows its more delicate sweetness to shine through. Vibrant green spinach and chopped walnuts add color and texture while the white wine butter sauce brings everything to life and places the delicious blue cheese front and center. This unique pasta dish pairs beautifully with a sweeter white wine, such as Sauternes.

PREP TIME: 15 minutes | **COOK TIME:** 15 minutes | **MAKES** 4 servings

MEAL: Lunch, Dinner

10 oz (283 g) mafaldine pasta, or similar dried pasta

3 tbsp (42 g) butter

3–4 cloves garlic, minced or pressed

5–6 fresh thyme sprigs, leaves picked, divided

3 oz (85 g) dried cranberries, roughly chopped

½ cup (125 ml) white wine or vegetable stock

4½ oz (128 g) baby spinach, roughly chopped

8 oz (226 g) blue cheese of choice, crumbled or roughly chopped, divided

¼ cup (29 g) walnuts, chopped

1. Bring a large pot of salted water to a boil. Add the pasta and cook until al dente, tender yet firm to the bite, according to the package directions. Reserve about ½ cup (120 ml) of the pasta water before draining. Drain well.

2. In a large skillet over medium-high heat, melt the butter. Add the garlic, 3 to 4 sprigs of the thyme leaves and cranberries. Cook for 1 to 2 minutes, or until fragrant.

3. Increase the heat to high, add the wine and cook for 2 to 3 minutes, or until mostly reduced. Stir in the spinach and cook until just wilted, for 1 to 2 minutes longer.

4. While the skillet is still on the heat, add the cooked pasta, reserved pasta water and 4 ounces (113 g) of the blue cheese. Keep cooking and tossing the pasta with tongs for 1 to 2 minutes, until the cheese melts and forms a sauce that coats the pasta.

5. Divide the pasta into bowls. Add the remaining 4 ounces (113 g) of the blue cheese on top and sprinkle with the walnuts and remaining thyme.

TIPS: *I used crumbly Stilton but you can substitute with Roquefort, Gorgonzola or Danish Blue. These will melt well into the pasta water and form a super delicious sauce.*

You can also substitute fresh cranberries but be sure to double the amount of dried cranberries if you do so.

You can make this recipe with other pasta such as tagliatelle, fettuccini or pappardelle.

TWICE-BAKED BUTTERNUT SQUASH WITH GORGONZOLA

Blue cheese fans will go gaga over this caramelized, sweet squash with a creamy filling, loaded with lots of salty and bold Gorgonzola cheese. Simple enough for a weeknight with only five ingredients, it's also elegant enough to serve for holiday dinners. Gorgonzola is a great entry-level blue cheese because it's milder than more prominently funky varieties. When it gets hot and toasty in the oven it transforms into a cheesy powerhouse. This vegetarian entree or side dish takes a simple fall vegetable to new heights. Serve with a matured dry white or red wine, such as Chenin Blanc or Merlot.

PREP TIME: 10 minutes | **COOK TIME:** 40–50 minutes | **MAKES** 4 servings

MEAL: Dinner

2 medium butternut squash, halved lengthwise and seeded

Sea salt and freshly ground black pepper, to taste

1 tbsp (15 ml) avocado or olive oil

10½ oz (298 g) plain Greek yogurt

8 oz (226 g) Gorgonzola, divided

1. Preheat the oven to 400°F (200°C). Line a sheet pan with parchment paper.

2. Place the halved butternut squash, cut side up, onto the prepared sheet pan and season with salt and pepper. Drizzle with the oil and use your fingers to spread it over the squash.

3. Transfer the pan to the preheated oven and bake for 40 to 50 minutes, or until fork-tender. Once the squash is done, remove from the oven and let it cool slightly, or until easy to handle.

4. In a large bowl, scoop out the flesh of a squash half with a spoon, leaving the skin intact to create a boat. Leave at least a ¼-inch (6-mm) border around the squash skin so it will retain its shape. Repeat with the remaining halves.

5. To the squash flesh, add the Greek yogurt, salt, pepper and 6 ounces (170 g) of the Gorgonzola. Mix until well combined. Spoon the mixture back into the squash boats. Top with the remaining 2 ounces (57 g) of the Gorgonzola.

6. Place the squash back in the preheated oven and bake for another 8 to 10 minutes, or until the cheese is melted and the squash is golden-brown on top. Set the oven to broil and cook for 2 to 3 minutes, or until the tops are golden.

BLUE MAC & CHEESE

Traditional mac and cheese is great, but more sophisticated cheese lovers will adore this fancy version that uses deliciously savory Gorgonzola. This blue-veined cheese has all of the great flavors of strong blue cheeses but is a little milder, making it a fantastic ingredient for cheese sauces. Sprinkling the finished dish with chopped walnuts adds crunch and another elegant touch. The winning feature of this dinner is that it's friendly enough to serve to kids but sophisticated enough for adults. Try serving it alongside a bold red wine, such as Cabernet Franc.

PREP TIME: 5 minutes | **COOK TIME:** 8-10 minutes | **MAKES** 4-6 servings

MEAL: Lunch, Dinner

12 oz (340 g) elbow macaroni

2 cups (480 ml) heavy cream

6 oz (170 g) Gorgonzola or Cashel, crumbled or chopped

Freshly grated nutmeg, to taste, plus more for garnishing

Kosher salt, to taste

4 oz (113 g) walnuts, coarsely chopped

1. Bring a large pot of salted water to a boil. Add the pasta and cook until al dente, tender yet firm to the bite, according to the package directions. Drain.

2. Meanwhile, place a saucepot over medium heat and add in the heavy cream and Gorgonzola. Bring to a simmer and cook, stirring occasionally, until the cheese is melted and the sauce is slightly thickened, for 8 to 10 minutes.

3. Season with the freshly grated nutmeg and salt, to taste.

4. When the macaroni is done and drained, add the cheese sauce and toss well to coat evenly.

5. Divide the mac and cheese among plates and sprinkle with the walnuts and more of the freshly grated nutmeg.

STILTON-STUFFED SWEET POTATO BOATS

Elevate the humble sweet potato by stuffing it with plenty of elegantly rich and complex Stilton cheese. Baked sweet potatoes can be a little boring and one-note, but you'll be amazed how salty, crumbled Stilton can transform them into something spectacular. Smoky bacon, creamy yogurt, nutty pecans and a few other simple-to-prepare ingredients provide more fun toppings for the sweet spuds. A good drizzle of tangy balsamic vinegar adds a zip of acidity to bring everything together. With the steaming, fluffy baked sweet potatoes and the cool, creamy blue cheese, these taters will be the biggest hit at any dinner party. Serve with a sweet red like Tawny Port.

PREP TIME: 10 minutes | **COOK TIME:** 1 hour | **MAKES** 4 servings
MEAL: Lunch, Dinner

4 medium sweet potatoes

1 tbsp (15 ml) olive oil, plus extra to drizzle

12 slices smoked bacon

Sea salt and freshly ground black pepper, to taste

2 cups (480 ml) Greek yogurt, full-fat recommended

5½ oz (156 g) Stilton, crumbled

1 cup (109 g) pecans, coarsely chopped

3 oz (85 g) dried cranberries

2 tbsp (30 ml) good-quality balsamic vinegar, or to taste

TIP: *Use an aged Balsamic of Modena vinegar, which is denser, sweeter and more flavorful than regular balsamic. It has a lower acidity and a more balanced sweet-and-sour taste.*

1. Preheat the oven to 375°F (190°C). Line two large sheet pans with parchment paper.

2. Scrub the potatoes under running cold water and pat dry with a paper towel.

3. Place the potatoes on one of the prepared sheet pans and pierce a few holes into each with a fork. Drizzle with the olive oil and, using your hands, rub the oil over the potatoes in a thin, even layer.

4. Transfer the pan to the middle rack of your preheated oven and bake for 40 minutes to 1 hour. Because potatoes vary in size, check for doneness after 40 minutes by stabbing them in the center with a knife. If it goes through easily, they're done. If not, return to the oven and bake for 10 to 20 minutes longer.

5. Meanwhile, arrange the bacon slices onto the second prepared sheet pan. Place in the oven and bake for 12 to 20 minutes or until golden-brown and crispy. The baking time will depend on how thick the bacon is and how crispy you like it. Keep an eye on the bacon while it bakes and check it after 10 minutes. When the bacon is cooked to your liking, remove from the sheet pan and place it on a paper towel–lined plate to absorb the excess grease. As soon as it cools, chop or crumble the bacon and set aside.

6. Once the potatoes are done, remove them from the oven and let them cool for about 15 minutes.

7. Using a sharp knife, carefully make a long cut along the top of each potato and open them gently. Using a fork, fluff up the soft, orange flesh. Sprinkle with a pinch of salt and pepper, to taste.

8. Top each potato with equal amounts of the yogurt, Stilton cheese, chopped pecans, crispy bacon and cranberries. Drizzle with a tiny bit of the olive oil and balsamic vinegar.

CREAMY ROQUEFORT CHICKEN GNOCCHI

Creamy Roquefort cheese has a strong but delicious flavor that becomes more mellow and tamed in cream sauces. In this chicken gnocchi dish, fresh potato gnocchi is broiled with seasoned chicken, fresh baby spinach and a cheesy cream sauce, laced with lots of funky Roquefort and sweet onion. With a golden-brown crust and bubbling cheesy sauce, this gnocchi meal is perfect for days when you need a big hug in the form of comfort food. Serve these cheesy potato dumplings with a dry white wine, such as Vermentino.

PREP TIME: 10 minutes | **COOK TIME:** 18–20 minutes | **MAKES** 4–5 servings
MEAL: Dinner

17½ oz (496 g) store-bought refrigerated gnocchi

1 lb (453 g) skinless, boneless chicken breasts

Sea salt and freshly ground black pepper, to taste

2 tbsp (30 ml) olive oil, divided

1 medium sweet onion, diced

2 cloves garlic, minced

1 red chili pepper, thinly sliced

1 cup (240 ml) heavy cream

Zest of 1 lemon

8 oz (226 g) Roquefort, crumbled

5 oz (142 g) baby spinach, washed and dried

1. Cook the gnocchi according to the package directions. After draining, place them in an oven-safe dish and set aside.

2. Meanwhile, season the chicken on both sides with salt and pepper.

3. In a large skillet, heat 1 tablespoon (15 ml) of the oil over medium heat. Add the chicken and cook for 5 to 7 minutes on each side, or until golden-brown and cooked through. Set aside on a chopping board to rest for a few minutes, then slice into strips.

4. Add the remaining 1 tablespoon (15 ml) of the oil to the same skillet and sauté the onion for 3 to 4 minutes, or until softened. Add the garlic and chili and cook, stirring continuously, for 1 minute longer.

5. With a wooden spoon, stir in the heavy cream, lemon zest and crumbled Roquefort. Stir until everything is well combined and the cheese is melted into the sauce. Add the spinach and stir until wilted.

6. Transfer the sliced chicken to the oven dish with the cooked gnocchi. Pour the Roquefort sauce on top and gently stir so everything is nicely coated in sauce. Season to taste with a pinch of salt and pepper.

7. Turn on the broiler and place the dish underneath the heat for 3 to 5 minutes, or until the tops are golden and the sauce is bubbly.

APPLE AND STILTON SALAD WITH ROASTED HAZELNUTS

Pairing blue cheese with sweet fruits is a great way to mellow some of the pungency of the cheese and offset some of its saltiness. Stilton is especially rich, and sweetening it with refreshingly crisp apple in a salad makes for one of the best combinations in existence. Tossing the salad with a sharp Dijon-shallot vinaigrette provides a wonderful tang that can stand up to the beautiful flavor of the cheese and complement its intensity. This flavorful salad may sound unassuming, but it certainly doesn't skimp on flavor! It pairs well with peppery red wines, such as Syrah.

PREP TIME: 15 minutes | **COOK TIME:** 10 minutes | **MAKES** 4–6 servings
MEAL: Appetizer, Side Dish

SALAD

1 cup (128 g) raw hazelnuts

4 ribs celery, cut into ¼-inch (6-mm) dice

3 large red delicious apples, cored and cut into ¼-inch (6-mm) dice

7 oz (198 g) Stilton, crumbled

DRESSING

2 tbsp (30 ml) apple cider vinegar

1 tbsp (15 g) minced shallot

1 tbsp (15 ml) Dijon mustard

Sea salt and freshly ground black pepper, to taste

4 tbsp (60 ml) extra virgin olive oil

1. Preheat the oven to 350°F (180°C).

2. Place the hazelnuts on a rimmed sheet pan and roast for 8 to 10 minutes, or until fragrant and slightly golden. Remove from the oven and let the hazelnuts cool for a bit, then coarsely chop them.

3. Meanwhile, to make the dressing, in a small jar, add all the dressing ingredients. Screw the lid on tightly and shake vigorously to emulsify.

4. In a medium bowl, add the diced celery and apples. Add the dressing, hazelnuts and Stilton. Gently toss to evenly coat and combine.

TIP: *Make more of the roasted hazelnuts because this dish goes perfectly with the Cauliflower Soup with Blue Cheese and Beetroot (page 84). Both recipes use roasted hazelnuts and blue cheese.*

BACON AND STILTON MASHED POTATOES

The combination of bacon and blue cheese is a classic—and for a good reason. The intensity of a blue cheese, such as Stilton, has enough flavor to stand up to the smokiness of the bacon without overpowering it. When mixed with the blank canvas of potatoes, the strong flavors of the bacon and blue cheese are tamed to elevate simple mashed potatoes into something extra special. Be sure to top the spuds with extra cheese and bacon for a pretty touch, as well as some crunch.

PREP TIME: 15 minutes | **COOK TIME:** 20 minutes | **MAKES** 8–10 servings

MEAL: Side Dish

9 oz (255 g) bacon, chopped

3 lbs (1.4 kg) Yukon gold potatoes, peeled and cubed

2 large cloves garlic, crushed

1½–2 cups (360–480 ml) water, or as needed

1 tsp sea salt, or to taste

10 oz (283 g) Stilton cheese, crumbled, divided

½ tsp freshly ground black pepper, or to taste

1 tbsp (4 g) fresh parsley, chopped

1. Place a pot or a Dutch oven over medium heat. Add in the chopped bacon and cook for 5 to 6 minutes, stirring frequently, until crispy. Set aside on a paper towel to absorb the excess grease.

2. Place the potatoes and garlic in the Dutch oven. Cover with the water to ½ inch (1.3 cm) above the potatoes. Season with the salt. Bring to a boil and once it starts to bubble, reduce the heat and simmer for 15 minutes, or until the potatoes are very tender.

3. When the potatoes are done, remove from the heat and discard the garlic cloves. Reserve half of the liquid in a cup and set aside. Drain the rest of the liquid from the potatoes.

4. In a food processor, add the potatoes and most of the Stilton, making sure to reserve some for garnishing.

5. Process until the mashed potatoes are smooth. Alternatively, transfer the potatoes to a large bowl and mash by hand with a potato masher.

6. Add some of the reserved liquid from the cooked potatoes to reach your desired consistency. Taste and season with more salt and pepper, as needed.

7. Transfer the mashed potatoes to a platter and top with the crispy bacon, reserved Stilton and parsley.

CAULIFLOWER SOUP WITH BLUE CHEESE AND BEETROOT

Even those who say they dislike blue cheese will want to dig right into this smooth and creamy cauliflower soup. The pungent flavors of the rich blue cheese are tamed, thanks to the sweeter notes from beetroot and pears. Topping with roasted hazelnuts gives the soup a gourmet finishing touch and further complements the funky blue cheese. This uniquely sweet-and-salty soup is full of surprising flavors that you'll find yourself craving time and time again.

PREP TIME: 15 minutes | **COOK TIME:** 40 minutes | **MAKES** 4-6 servings
MEAL: Lunch, Dinner

1 cup (128 g) raw hazelnuts

10 oz (283 g) smoked, cured bacon slices

3 tbsp (42 g) unsalted butter

1 small red onion, peeled and diced

1 small to medium cauliflower head, broken into florets

1 (1-lb [454-g]) pack of steamed beetroot (whole, peeled, cooked and ready to eat)

3 medium pears, peeled, cored and roughly chopped

5 cups (1.2 L) low-sodium vegetable stock

Sea salt and freshly ground black pepper, to taste

6 oz (170 g) blue cheese of choice (see Tip), roughly chopped, divided

1 tsp dried chives, for garnishing

Crusty bread, for serving (optional)

TIP: *This soup makes a great appetizer before the Apple and Stilton Salad with Roasted Hazelnuts (page 80). I used a blue Stilton for this recipe, but you can also use mild Danish Blue, the more pungent Roquefort or a Gorgonzola variety.*

1. Preheat the oven to 320°F (160°C). Line two sheet pans with parchment paper.

2. Arrange the hazelnuts in a single layer on one of the prepared sheet pans and transfer to the preheated oven. Roast for 12 to 15 minutes. Shake the pan a couple of times during cooking to ensure the hazelnuts roast evenly. You'll know they're done when their skins crack and they start to release their wonderful nutty fragrance.

3. Remove the hazelnuts from the oven and allow to cool.

4. Arrange the bacon slices in a single layer on the second sheet pan. Bake in the preheated oven for 12 to 15 minutes, or until the bacon is crispy. Once the bacon is done, transfer to a paper towel–lined plate to absorb the excess fat.

5. Meanwhile, in a large saucepot over medium heat, melt the butter. Add the onion and sauté for 4 to 5 minutes, or until softened.

6. Stir in the cauliflower florets, beetroot and pears. Cover with the stock. Bring to a boil and as soon as it starts bubbling, reduce the heat and simmer for 15 to 20 minutes, or until the cauliflower and pears are tender.

7. Remove from the heat and, using a hand blender, blend until smooth. Taste and adjust the seasonings, if needed. You could also transfer to a blender in batches and blend until smooth.

8. While the soup is hot, stir in most of the blue cheese, making sure to reserve some for garnishing.

9. Ladle the soup into serving bowls and top with reserved blue cheese. Crumble the crispy bacon on top and sprinkle with the hazelnuts and dried chives. Serve with the crusty bread if desired.

BUFFALO CHEESE BALL WITH CRUMBLED STILTON

There's nothing quite like the blue cheese that gives buffalo wings their signature flavor. In this spicy buffalo chicken–inspired cheese ball, tangy cream cheese serves as the base for a smooth and creamy spread, while crumbled blue cheese provides a salty, strong punch that is absolutely necessary for this American classic. Using store-bought buffalo sauce, this party appetizer comes together in the blink of an eye.

PREP TIME: 15 minutes plus inactive time for refrigerating the cheese ball | **MAKES** 8–10 servings

MEAL: Appetizer

2 tbsp (28 g) unsalted butter, softened

1 mild red chili pepper, seeded and chopped

1 clove garlic, minced

8 oz (226 g) cream cheese, at room temperature

2 tbsp (30 ml) Buffalo hot sauce

3½ oz (100 g) blue cheese of choice, crumbled

1 rib celery, finely diced

3 tbsp (9 g) chopped chives

Kosher salt and freshly ground black pepper, to taste

4 oz (113 g) walnuts, chopped

Assorted crackers, celery and carrot sticks, for serving

1. In a small saucepan over medium heat, add the butter. Once it's sizzling, toss in the chili and garlic. Sauté, stirring constantly for about 1 minute or until the garlic is fragrant. Remove from the heat and set aside to cool.

2. In a mixing bowl, add the cream cheese and Buffalo sauce. Beat using a hand mixer until smooth.

3. Add the chili-garlic butter, blue cheese, celery, chives and a pinch of salt and pepper. Using a spatula, stir until well combined. Taste and adjust the seasonings, if needed.

4. Place a large piece of plastic wrap onto a clean work surface. Add the cheese mixture to the middle and wrap with the plastic, using your hands to form it into a ball shape.

5. Refrigerate for 2 to 3 hours, until firm.

6. When ready to serve, place the walnuts in a shallow dish. Unwrap the cheese ball and roll it in the walnuts until the outside is evenly coated. Place on a platter and serve with the crackers, celery and carrot sticks.

TIP: *I used a blue Stilton for this recipe but you can also make it with other types of crumbly matured blue cheese such as Danish Blue, Roquefort or Mountain Gorgonzola.*

GOUDA, GRUYÈRE, CHEDDAR, HALLOUMI & PROVOLONE

Sharp Yet Not Too Tangy Meals with Semi-Firm Cheeses

Firm and semi-firm cheeses, such as Gouda, Gruyère, Cheddar, halloumi and provolone, have the perfect balance between savory and tangy. Even though they contain less moisture than softer varieties, they still have a relatively mild flavor, with plenty of rich, buttery notes. These cheeses are great for slicing and grating, as well as for serving in large chunks like in my Mediterranean Cobb Salad with Fried Halloumi (page 98).

Usually aged for a relatively short amount of time, firm and semi-firm cheeses develop a sharp flavor but they don't have the intense tang of harder cheeses, such as pecorino. These cheeses are extremely versatile. They have the melting properties of younger cheeses and the complex, nutty flavors of aged cheese.

Firm and semi-firm cheeses are perhaps the most widely available cheeses on the market because they range from very young and mild to aged and intense in flavor. For example, Cheddar can be found in many different varieties. The mild version is softer and more buttery than other varieties and melts wonderfully, making it great for cheese sauces or for melting on top of casseroles. Sharp Cheddar is aged longer and has a smooth, slightly crumbly texture with an intense tangy flavor. A sharp variety can be substituted in a recipe calling for a mild Cheddar but it will be less melty and have a stronger flavor. Other premium Cheddars are aged longer than sharp Cheddar and have an intense flavor, along with some nuttiness. These are great for cheese boards and they pair wonderfully with meats and wine.

Other cheeses that can vary in flavor and texture are Gouda and Gruyère. Gouda, from Holland, has many different varieties and is categorized by age. Young Gouda is soft, mild and slightly sweet, making it great for sandwiches. Aged Gouda develops a stronger, richer flavor with notes of butter and toasted nuts. With a more pronounced flavor, these are great in my Smoky Mac & Cheese (page 105) and on The Classic Cheese Platter (page 142). Gruyère, originally from Switzerland, also has many varieties. Its base characteristics are sweetness, nuttiness and a slight saltiness, plus it's one of the most popular melting cheeses. Gruyère tends to be milder than other cheeses, making it extremely versatile. Try using it in fondue or in a delicious croque monsieur.

In this chapter, you'll learn how to give familiar foods a sophisticated upgrade with these complex firm and semi-firm cheeses. While we all love the classics, devoted cheese lovers know it's important to change things up with more flavorful cheeses whenever possible. So, get yourself a nice, cold pilsner while you explore some beautiful recipes using firm and semi-firm cheeses.

PHILLY CHEESE STEAK SKILLET WITH PROVOLONE

This easy take on the Philly cheese steak is made in one skillet for a simple meal and is loaded with meaty, cheesy goodness. Searing a good cut of steak in a hot pan allows the crust to become nicely charred while retaining a juicy, pink center. Sautéing garlic, peppers and onions in the same pan infuses them with the strong meaty flavors, essential for a good Philly cheese steak. A generous portion of melty provolone or Cheddar is the icing on the cake. After some time on the stove, the cheese becomes hot and bubbly, turning this meal from good to great. Serve with a full-bodied Cabernet Sauvignon.

PREP TIME: 15 minutes | **COOK TIME:** 15 minutes | **MAKES** 4 servings
MEAL: Dinner

1½ lbs (626 g) beef steak (e.g., rib eye, sirloin or top sirloin)

Sea salt and freshly ground black pepper, to taste

2 tbsp (28 g) butter, divided

1 tbsp (15 ml) olive oil

1 large sweet onion, sliced

2 cloves garlic, minced or pressed

3 large mixed-color peppers, cut into matchsticks

1 tbsp (15 ml) chili pepper or hot sauce, or to taste

2 tbsp (30 ml) Worcestershire sauce

1 cup (128 g) provolone cheese, freshly grated

2 tbsp (8 g) fresh parsley, chopped, for garnishing

1. Remove the steak from the refrigerator and season on both sides with a pinch of salt and pepper. Allow it to come to room temperature for about 15 minutes.

2. In a large skillet over medium heat, melt 1 tablespoon (14 g) of the butter. Add the steak and cook for 4 to 5 minutes, flipping it every 2 minutes or so for medium-rare doneness. Cooking times may vary depending on the thickness of your cut of steak. Remove to a plate and loosely cover with aluminum foil to allow the meat to rest.

3. In the same skillet, add the remaining 1 tablespoon (14 g) of the butter, oil, onion, garlic and peppers. Add the chili sauce and Worcestershire sauce. Stir-fry for 3 to 4 minutes, until the vegetables are crisp-tender.

4. Meanwhile, slice the steak and add it to the skillet. Stir in the cheese.

5. Cover the skillet with a lid and cook for 1 to 2 minutes, until the cheese is melted.

6. Remove to a serving platter and garnish with the parsley.

TIPS: *Use a good beef cut such as rib eye, sirloin, top sirloin or T-bone. Be careful not to overcook the steak as it will continue to cook while it rests and when you return it to the skillet while the cheese melts.*

If you don't have provolone on hand, I suggest using a milder flavor cheese, such as a mild Cheddar instead of a sharp variety, so it doesn't overpower the steak's flavor.

CRISPY HALLOUMI "FRIES" WITH ROASTED TOMATO DIP

Squeaky halloumi cheese holds up tremendously well on the griddle and makes a fun, new twist on french fries. With a salty, mild flavor, Greek halloumi is great for serving in large quantities as the main event. Coat the sticks of cheese in a smoky, seasoned flour mixture and then fry until crispy. A sauce made with roasted cherry tomatoes and lots of garlic is the perfect dip for the salty cheese sticks. Think of this dish as mozzarella sticks and marinara sauce but with a bigger punch of flavor. These sophisticated cheese sticks are tons of fun to eat! Serve it with a medium acidity white wine, such as Chenin Blanc.

PREP TIME: 15 minutes | **COOK TIME:** 25–30 minutes | **MAKES** 4 servings
MEAL: Snack, Appetizer

ROASTED TOMATO DIP

17½ oz (496 g) grape or cherry tomatoes

10–12 cloves garlic, or to taste

2 tbsp (30 ml) extra virgin olive oil

½ tsp chili powder

½ tsp sea salt, or to taste

¼ tsp freshly ground black pepper, or to taste

HALLOUMI "FRIES"

16 oz (454 g) halloumi cheese

½ cup (63 g) all-purpose flour

2 tsp (1 g) smoked paprika

1 tsp onion powder

1 tsp dried oregano

2–3 tbsp (30–45 ml) sunflower or avocado oil, for frying

Small bunch fresh parsley, chopped, for garnishing

1. Preheat the oven to 400°F (200°C).

2. To make the roasted tomato dip, in a mixing bowl, combine all the dip ingredients. Toss until nicely coated. Transfer to a baking dish.

3. Place the dish in the preheated oven and roast for 25 to 30 minutes, or until the tomatoes are charred on the top.

4. Meanwhile, prepare the halloumi "fries." Start by cutting the halloumi cheese into ½-inch (1.3-cm)-thick sticks.

5. In a bowl or a shallow dish, mix the flour, paprika, onion powder and oregano until well combined. Add a few pieces of the halloumi cheese at a time and lightly, but evenly, coat them with the flour mixture. Shake to remove any excess flour.

6. In a large skillet over medium heat, heat the oil. Add the halloumi "fries" and cook until golden on all sides, for 4 to 5 minutes total. Use a pair of tongs to turn them so they cook on all sides.

7. To get a crispy exterior, don't overcrowd the skillet. Work in batches of 8 to 10 "fries" per batch. Transfer the "fries" to a paper towel to absorb any excess fat.

8. When the roasted tomatoes are done, transfer all the contents, including the juices, to a blender. Blend until the mixture turns into a chunky dip. Taste the dip and adjust the seasoning to your taste.

9. Arrange the halloumi "fries" on a large platter and place the dip in the middle. Sprinkle with the parsley.

CHEESY CHICKEN CROQUETTES WITH SHARP CHEDDAR

The presence of leftover chicken should never be dreaded, thanks to dishes such as these cheesy chicken croquettes. Sharp Cheddar is the perfect balance between melty and fully flavored, turning plain chicken from bland to bold in this tasty appetizer. Seasoned breadcrumbs and a light fry in avocado oil give these cheesy snacks a crispy, crunchy crust, with a soft and melty inside. Serve these with a full-bodied white wine, such as Chardonnay.

PREP TIME: 15 minutes | **COOK TIME:** 10 minutes | **MAKES** 4–5 servings (about 20 croquettes)

MEAL: Snack, Appetizer

9 oz (255 g) chicken, cooked and thinly shredded

9 oz (255 g) sharp Cheddar, shredded

¼ cup (27 g) seasoned breadcrumbs

2 large eggs

3 tbsp (9 g) chives, chopped

½ tsp chili flakes, or to taste

1 tsp smoked paprika

1 tsp garlic powder

2 tbsp (30 ml) avocado or vegetable oil, for frying

1. In a large bowl, add the chicken, Cheddar, breadcrumbs, eggs, chives, chili flakes, paprika and garlic powder. Mix thoroughly to combine.

2. Using your hands, take a spoonful of the chicken mixture and roll it between your palms to create a ball-shaped croquette. Repeat with the remaining mixture.

3. Heat a large nonstick pan over medium heat. Add the oil. Cook the chicken croquettes in one layer, making sure not to overcrowd the pan.

4. Cook for 5 to 6 minutes, until golden and crispy on all sides. Serve with your favorite dip.

TIPS: *Shred the chicken as thinly as possible, or use a very sharp knife to chop it. Alternatively, you can place the pieces of cooked chicken in a food processor and pulse until they are fully shredded.*

If you only have plain breadcrumbs, add 1 teaspoon of Italian seasoning and mix to combine.

BROCC & CHEESE

With this elevated casserole made using Cheddar and Gruyère, children and adults alike will be pleased. Tangy sharp Cheddar is a flavorful step up from an average mild Cheddar, especially when paired with the sweeter, nutty Gruyère. Laced with a hint of grated nutmeg, these two melting cheeses shine in a homemade, comfortingly creamy sauce that is a must-try for any cheese lover. Because blanching the broccoli before baking the casserole is an optional step, this bake is great for weeknight meal planning as it can be made in about 40 minutes. Serve with a well-rounded citrusy red wine, such as Sémillon.

PREP TIME: 10 minutes | **COOK TIME:** 30 minutes | **MAKES** 4–5 servings

MEAL: Lunch, Dinner

Cooking oil spray

2 tbsp (28 g) butter, divided

2 tbsp (16 g) gluten-free all-purpose flour blend

2 cups (480 ml) whole milk

8 oz (226 g) sharp Cheddar cheese, shredded

4½ oz (128 g) Gruyère, shredded

½ tsp nutmeg, ground

¾ tsp onion powder

Sea salt and freshly ground black pepper, to taste

¼ cup (27 g) seasoned breadcrumbs

½ tsp garlic powder

2 lbs (907 g) broccoli, broken into small florets

1. Preheat the oven to 375°F (190°C). Lightly grease a 9 x 13–inch (23 x 33–cm) baking dish with cooking oil spray.

2. In a small pot over medium heat, melt 1 tablespoon (14 g) of the butter. Stir in the flour and cook, whisking continuously, for about 1 minute.

3. Gradually pour in the milk, whisking well to dissolve any lumps.

4. Bring the milk mixture to a boil. Reduce the heat and simmer for 4 to 5 minutes, stirring often, until thickened.

5. Remove the pot from the heat and stir in the Cheddar, Gruyère, nutmeg, onion powder, salt and pepper. Mix well until the cheese is melted and fully incorporated into the sauce.

6. In a large, heavy skillet over medium heat, melt the remaining 1 tablespoon (14 g) of the butter. Add the breadcrumbs and garlic powder. Stir with a wooden spoon and cook until golden, about 2 minutes. Transfer to a bowl and set aside.

7. Place the broccoli florets into the prepared baking dish. Pour the cheese sauce on top and lightly stir to blend. Sprinkle the breadcrumbs on top.

8. Bake in the preheated oven for 18 to 20 minutes, or until the broccoli is tender and the sauce is bubbly.

TIPS: *Make sure to use a gluten-free flour blend with tapioca or cornstarch added, as this helps thicken your sauce better than regular flour.*

If you have problems digesting broccoli, you can steam or blanch the florets before adding them to the sauce. If you do, make sure to reduce the baking time to 8 to 12 minutes, or until the broccoli is tender. You can also replace the broccoli with cauliflower and follow the recipe just the same.

If you only have plain breadcrumbs, add 1 teaspoon of Italian seasoning and mix to combine.

MEDITERRANEAN COBB SALAD WITH FRIED HALLOUMI

Fried halloumi cheese makes this colorful Cobb salad something you'll want in your regular rotation. In this Mediterranean take on the classic, romaine lettuce is coated in a punchy red wine vinaigrette and topped with artfully arranged cucumber chunks, spicy salami, sweet cherry tomatoes, briny olives, hard-boiled eggs and the squeaky fried halloumi. Reminiscent of cheese curds, the fried halloumi with a golden-brown crust adds a uniquely salty element to the salad. This cheesy Cobb salad looks like a rainbow on a plate. Suggested wine pairings include a tangy white, such as Sauvignon Blanc, or a light red, such as Pinot Noir.

PREP TIME: 15 minutes | **COOK TIME:** 18 minutes | **MAKES** 4 servings

MEAL: Lunch, Dinner

DRESSING

3 tbsp (45 ml) extra virgin olive oil

2 tbsp (30 ml) red wine vinegar

1 small clove garlic, pressed or minced (or ½ tsp garlic powder)

1 tbsp (15 ml) Dijon mustard

1 tsp dried oregano

¼ tsp freshly ground black pepper

½ tsp fine sea salt

SALAD

4 large eggs

12 oz (340 g) halloumi cheese

1 tbsp (15 ml) avocado or vegetable oil, for frying

5 oz (142 g) romaine leaves, washed and spin-dried

1 English cucumber, peeled and diced

10½ oz (298 g) cherry or grape tomatoes, quartered

3 oz (85 g) salami, chopped

6 oz (170 g) mixed Greek or Italian olives

1. To make the dressing, in a small bowl, whisk all the dressing ingredients together and set aside.

2. In a medium saucepan, carefully add the whole eggs to the bottom of the pan. Cover the eggs with cold water by about 1 inch (2.5 cm). Bring to a boil over medium-high heat.

3. Once the water starts bubbling, reduce the heat and simmer on low for about 12 minutes. Drain and rinse the eggs under cold water until they're cool enough to handle. Peel and coarsely chop the eggs and set aside.

4. Slice the halloumi cheese into bite-size cubes.

5. Heat a large skillet over medium-high heat. Add the oil and heat until shimmering.

6. Carefully place the halloumi cheese cubes in the hot oil. Fry, undisturbed, for 3 to 4 minutes. Flip the cubes and cook for a few minutes longer or until golden-brown. Set aside.

7. In a large serving bowl, mix the romaine with the dressing, tossing until evenly coated. Arrange the chopped eggs, fried halloumi, cucumber, tomatoes, salami and olives in rows on top.

CHEESY HASH BROWNS WITH RED CHEDDAR AND PROVOLONE

Crispy potatoes always taste better with the addition of cheese. Red Cheddar, also known as red Leicester, is the highlight of this cheesy potato dish. An English cheese, traditionally dyed red, is often found today as a white or yellow cheese with a red wax coating. It tastes like a mild Cheddar—but with a richer flavor—and can be substituted with mild Cheddar. In this craveable breakfast dish, a creamy potato mixture, loaded with red Cheddar and melty provolone, is layered in a pan, stuffed with more cheese and baked until crispy and golden-brown. The crisp, buttery exterior and ooey-gooey, cheese-filled center will have you planning a second batch before you finish enjoying the first.

PREP TIME: 15 minutes | **COOK TIME:** 35 minutes | **MAKES** 5 servings

MEAL: Breakfast, Lunch, Dinner

4 oz (113 g) red Cheddar or Monterey Jack, shredded, divided

5½ oz (156 g) provolone cheese, shredded, divided

20 oz (567 g) potatoes, shredded

2 tbsp (6 g) chives, chopped

6–8 fresh thyme sprigs, leaves picked

Sea salt and freshly ground black pepper, to taste

1½ cups (360 ml) heavy cream

1 large egg

1 red chili pepper, seeded and chopped

1–2 cloves garlic, minced

2 tbsp (28 g) butter or ghee

1. Preheat the oven to 400°F (200°C).

2. In a large bowl, combine about three-fourths of the red Cheddar with about three-fourths of the provolone cheese. Add the potatoes, chives, thyme, salt and pepper. Mix well.

3. In a second bowl, whisk the double cream with the egg, chili and garlic. Add a pinch of salt and pepper to taste. Whisk until well combined and smooth.

4. Pour the egg mixture over the potato and cheese mixture. Stir to combine.

5. In a large oven-safe skillet over medium-high heat, melt the butter. Once the skillet is hot and the butter starts bubbling, add the hash brown mixture. Use a wooden spoon to make an even layer in the skillet.

6. Sprinkle the remaining red Cheddar and provolone cheese on top. Transfer the skillet to the middle rack of the preheated oven.

7. Bake for 45 to 55 minutes, or until golden-brown on top and crispy on the edges.

8. Remove from the oven and carefully divide onto plates.

AVOCADO AND GOUDA-STUFFED FRENCH TOAST

Nutty, buttery Gouda plays well with the creamy avocado and sweet onion relish in this savory stuffed French toast. Gouda has a wide range of styles, so I recommend a good aged cheese for a strong flavor. However, a milder one for a delicate hint of cheesiness is just fine, if you prefer. After a dip in an egg mixture and frying on the griddle, the bread becomes nice and toasted with a melty, cheese-filled center.

PREP TIME: 15 minutes | **COOK TIME:** 6 minutes | **MAKES** 4 servings

MEAL: Breakfast, Lunch

4 large eggs

3 tbsp (45 ml) milk

½ tsp onion powder

¾ tsp sea salt, or to taste

¼ tsp freshly ground black pepper, or to taste

8 bread slices, about 1 inch (2.5 cm) thick

6 oz (170 g) onion relish

16 slices of Gouda

2 large ripe avocados, peeled, pitted and sliced

2 tbsp (28 g) salted butter

2 tbsp (30 ml) honey, for serving (optional)

1. In a shallow dish, whisk together the eggs, milk, onion powder, salt and pepper. Set aside.

2. Lay 2 slices of the bread on a cutting board and evenly spread a spoonful of the onion relish onto each.

3. Add 2 slices of Gouda to each. Add half of the sliced avocado on one bread slice, then sandwich the 2 bread slices together. Repeat the process with the remaining ingredients until you have four sandwiches ready for grilling.

4. Brush the butter on a griddle pan and place it over medium-low heat.

5. Add the sandwiches to the egg mixture, quickly dipping both sides until evenly coated.

6. Place on the preheated griddle and cook until the bread turns golden and the cheese is melted, 2 to 3 minutes per side.

7. Slice the sandwiches in half diagonally and drizzle with the honey, if using.

TIP: *I used pre-sliced Gouda cheese from a local deli shop, but you can also slice it at home if you have an entire block.*

SMOKY MAC & CHEESE

Give standard mac and cheese an upgrade with a warm and complex smoky flavor. Smoked Cheddar gives lusciously creamy cheese sauce a bold flavor, which is further enhanced by the smoked paprika. Fold the sauce with bite-size, al dente penne pasta and top with freshly toasted, seasoned breadcrumbs for a delicious crunch. This wonderfully smoky, uber-cheesy mac and cheese makes itself at home with any barbecued meat.

PREP TIME: 5 minutes | **COOK TIME:** 30 minutes | **MAKES** 6 servings

MEAL: Lunch, Dinner

3 tbsp (42 g) butter, divided

2 tbsp (18 g) gluten-free all-purpose flour blend

1 tbsp (7 g) smoked paprika

¾ tsp ground nutmeg

2½ cups (600 ml) whole milk

2 cups (226 g) smoked Cheddar, shredded

¼ cup (27 g) breadcrumbs (gluten-free if needed)

¼ tsp garlic powder

½ tsp Italian seasoning

1 lb (454 g) mini penne pasta (gluten-free if needed)

1. Preheat the oven to 375°F (190°C).

2. In a medium saucepan over medium heat, melt 2 tablespoons (28 g) of the butter. Add the flour and stir until the mixture turns golden, 3 to 4 minutes.

3. Add the paprika and nutmeg. Gradually whisk in the milk. Bring to a gentle boil and then immediately lower the heat. Simmer for about 4 minutes, stirring often, until the sauce thickens.

4. Once the sauce has thickened and can coat the back of a spoon, stir in the cheese and whisk until melted and smooth. Set aside.

5. In a small skillet over medium-high heat, melt the remaining 1 tablespoon (14 g) of butter. Add the breadcrumbs, garlic powder and Italian seasoning. Stir and cook for about 2 minutes, or until golden. Transfer to a plate.

6. Bring a large pot of salted water to a boil. Add the pasta and cook until al dente, tender yet firm to the bite, according to the package directions (see Tips below). Drain well. Pour the cheese sauce over the pasta and toss well to coat.

7. Divide among six 1¼-cup (300-ml) ramekins or oven dishes. Sprinkle with the breadcrumb mixture. Alternatively, you can use a 9 x 13-inch (23 x 33-cm) baking dish. Bake for 10 to 12 minutes, until bubbly and golden.

TIPS: *Undercook the pasta! If the package says 6 to 8 minutes for al dente, go for 5 to 6 minutes. This way, when baked with the sauce it won't become overcooked and mushy.*

Make sure to use a gluten-free flour blend with tapioca or cornstarch, as this helps thicken your sauce better than regular flour.

PARMIGIANO-REGGIANO, GRANA PADANO & PECORINO ROMANO

Rich, Savory Meals with Decadent Hard-Grating Cheeses

Hard-grating cheeses are a great way to deliver a roundhouse kick to your favorite foods. A little goes a long way. They tend to have a good amount of salt and umami flavors, giving your dishes a little "something something" that you just don't get from regular table salt. Hard cheeses have a lower moisture content than softer cheeses. Although they won't provide the cheesepull that melty mozzarella provides, they more than make up for it in flavor and texture. During that wonderful aging time, the flavor concentrates and the cheese take on a crumbly texture, with little crystals that provide crunch and sharpness.

Most people are familiar with Parmesan, a hard cheese made from a mixture of semi-skimmed and whole cow's milk, and its wide range of uses. As with many cheeses, there are cheaper types and expensive varieties. With Parmesan, you get what you pay for. You'll know you're getting the best Parmesan when it is labeled "Parmigiano-Reggiano." There are strict laws and quality tests the cheese must undergo to receive this label. Because this cheese is higher in quality, it has a stronger flavor and should be used when it is the main ingredient of a recipe. The rind can be used in the base of a soup to provide a rich, salty flavor. The more inexpensive Parmesans are great for adding to soups, pastas and other recipes where the dish has other bold flavors going on.

Grana Padano is another hard-grating cheese that is widely available. Think of it as a Parmesan that is less salty and nutty, with a lower fat content. There are fewer regulations that allow a cheese to be labeled "Grana Padano" than there are for "Parmesan" so its flavor can vary, depending on where the milk used to make the cheese is from. In general, Grana Padano is milder than Parmesan, so it's best used as an ingredient to add to dishes where you don't want it to overpower the other flavors in the dish.

Pecorino is another glorious hard-grating cheese that is arguably underused in countries outside of Italy. Because it is made from sheep's milk, rather than cow's milk, it has a tangy brightness. It is also a bit saltier and stronger in flavor than Parmesan. Pecorino can easily overpower a dish, so it's best used when you want the cheese to be one of the main flavors or when it's paired with jam on a cheese board. When you want a sharp, strong, cheesy flavor, pecorino is a great addition.

In this chapter, you'll find that hard cheeses are not only for topping pasta. They can hide in the background of a dish to provide subtle, cheesy nuances or they can be front and center, as part of the main event. Buckle up and let the glorious wheels of hard-grating cheese take you on a wild, flavor-packed ride.

PEAR AND PECORINO SALAD

Salty Pecorino Romano cheese is Parmesan's more assertive, tangier cousin. Made from sheep's milk and aged for a shorter amount of time than Parmesan, it has a more pungent flavor that works wonders in a salad with sweet, ripe pears. Toss mixed greens with hearty chickpeas, peppery chunks of Pecorino Romano, juicy chopped pears, tart pomegranate arils, toasted pine nuts and a white wine shallot vinaigrette for an elegant, yet simple appetizer. Fruit and cheese just got a sophisticated upgrade! Pair this sweet-and-salty salad with a light white wine, such as Pinot Grigio or Sauvignon Blanc.

PREP TIME: 15 minutes | **COOK TIME:** 3 minutes | **MAKES** 4 servings

MEAL: Lunch, Appetizer, Side Dish

DRESSING

¼ cup (60 ml) extra virgin olive oil

2 tbsp (30 ml) white wine vinegar

1 tbsp (15 ml) lemon juice, freshly squeezed

2 tsp (10 ml) pure maple syrup or honey

1 tbsp (15 ml) Dijon mustard

1 small shallot, grated

1 clove garlic, minced

Kosher salt and freshly ground black pepper, to taste

SALAD

½ cup (68 g) pine nuts

10 oz (283 g) mixed leafy greens

1 (15-oz [425-g]) can chickpeas, rinsed and drained

12 oz (340 g) Pecorino Romano, cut into bite-size pieces

2 ripe pears, cored and chopped

1 large pomegranate, seeded

Freshly ground black pepper, to taste

1. To make the dressing, in a small jar, add all the dressing ingredients. Screw the lid on tightly and shake vigorously to emulsify. Set aside.

2. Heat a nonstick pan over low heat. Add the pine nuts and toast, stirring frequently, for 2 to 3 minutes, or until the pine nuts are golden in spots. Remove to a plate and set aside.

3. In a large bowl, toss the greens, chickpeas, Pecorino Romano, pears and pomegranate.

4. Pour the prepared dressing over the salad and gently toss to coat. Sprinkle with the toasted pine nuts and add pepper to taste.

GRANA PADANO BEEF MEATBALLS IN TOMATO SAUCE

Cheese-infused beef meatballs with homemade tomato sauce are a Sunday family favorite. Hearty ground beef, plenty of fresh herbs, garlic and salty Grana Padano turn average meatballs into something extraordinary. The Grana Padano gives them that special something that adds so much depth of flavor without overpowering the herbs and beef. Finishing the meatballs in a hearty tomato sauce with more cheese makes them extra juicy and tender. Serve the succulent, cheesy meatballs with crusty bread and a rich red wine, such as Cabernet Sauvignon or Merlot, for a comforting, yet simple-to-make weeknight supper.

PREP TIME: 15 minutes | **COOK TIME:** 25 minutes | **MAKES** 4 servings
MEAL: Dinner

MEATBALLS

1½ lbs (680 g) ground beef

4½ oz (128 g) Grana Padano, finely grated

3 tbsp (10 g) fresh mixed herbs of choice (e.g., rosemary, basil, parsley or thyme), chopped

1–2 cloves garlic, minced

1 large egg

Sea salt and freshly ground black pepper, to taste

2 tbsp (30 ml) olive or avocado oil

TOMATO SAUCE

1 onion, diced

6 cloves garlic, crushed

14½ oz (411 g) tomatoes, diced with liquid

Sea salt and freshly ground pepper, to taste

¼ cup (25 g) Grana Padano, shaved or grated

Freshly chopped parsley or other herbs of choice, for garnishing

Crusty bread, for serving (optional)

1. To make the meatballs, in a large bowl, combine the ground beef, Grana Padano, herbs, garlic and egg. Sprinkle with salt and pepper. Using a wooden spoon, mix well to combine.

2. Using your damp hands, take a spoonful of the mixture and roll it between your palms to create a round meatball. Repeat with the remaining meat mixture.

3. In a large skillet, heat the oil over medium heat. Add the meatballs and cook until golden-brown on all sides, 4 to 5 minutes in total. Don't cook them all the way through as they will continue to cook in the sauce. Set aside on a plate.

4. To make the tomato sauce, in the same heated skillet, add the onion and sauté for 3 to 4 minutes, or until soft and translucent. Stir in the crushed garlic and cook for 1 minute, until just fragrant.

5. Add in the diced tomatoes and reduce the heat. Simmer for 5 minutes until all the flavors meld. Taste and season with salt and freshly ground pepper, as needed.

6. Carefully add the meatballs back to the skillet, one by one, nestling them into the sauce.

7. Cover the skillet and reduce the heat. Simmer for 12 to 15 minutes, or until the meatballs are cooked through and the sauce has thickened.

8. Remove from the heat and sprinkle with the Grana Padano, herbs and pepper. Serve with the crusty bread, if desired.

TIP: *For this recipe you can use either Grana Padano or Parmigiano-Reggiano.*

SAVORY CHILI AND GRANA PADANO COOKIES

Cheesy, savory cookies, similar to biscuits in the UK, are already a popular appetizer, but sharp Grana Padano takes them to an entirely new level. Gluten-free oat flour is mixed into light yet rich and buttery morsels that are loaded with herbs, spicy chili and the addictively salty cheese. The toasty cookie flavor is enhanced with the Grana Padano, making it a perfect pairing for dessert wines, such as Moscato or Riesling. All you'll need is a glass of wine, a plate of these guys and a good TV show to have the perfect night in.

PREP TIME: 10 minutes | **COOK TIME:** 25 minutes | **MAKES** 12 biscuits or 4 servings
MEAL: Snack, Appetizer

1¼ cups (156 g) oat flour (ground oats)

⅓ cup (75 g) unsalted butter, cubed

½ cup (50 g) Grana Padano, finely grated

1½ tbsp (5 g) dried chives, or other dried herbs of choice

1 tsp chili flakes, or to taste

½ tsp sea salt

1. In a mixing bowl, add the oat flour and butter. Use your fingers to mix and crumble the mixture.

2. Add the Grana Padano, chives, chili flakes and sea salt. Using your hands, mix well to turn the dry mixture into a dough. Place the dough on a large piece of plastic wrap and wrap it tightly. Refrigerate for about an hour.

3. Heat the oven to 360°F (180°C). Line a sheet pan with parchment paper.

4. Remove the chilled dough from the refrigerator. Divide into individual balls by taking a spoonful of dough and rolling it between your palms to form a small ball. You should have approximately 12 balls.

5. Place the balls onto the prepared sheet pan, leaving about 1 inch (2.5 cm) between them. With the back of a fork, gently press down on the center of each ball to flatten it.

6. Bake for 12 to 15 minutes until they turn golden-brown. Once the biscuits are done, remove from the oven and cool on a wire rack.

TIP: *There are three types of Grana Padano you can use to make these biscuits, and each one will have quite an impact on the taste.*

- *Grana Padano (aged 9 to 16 months): hard texture, slightly grainy, mild taste.*
- *Grana Padano Oltre 16 Mesi (aged more than 16 months): crumblier texture, more pronounced taste.*
- *Grana Padano Riserva (aged more than 20 months): grainy, crumbly, full flavored.*

For the best flavor, and if your budget allows as the price rises proportionately with the aging time, I suggest the Grana Padano Riserva.

CHILI PARMESAN SWEET POTATO SOUP

Creamy soups are the optimal way to use up leftover Parmesan rinds that you never know what to do with. Steeping the rinds in broth softens them and infuses the liquid with a mysteriously complex umami flavor. In this Chili Parmesan Sweet Potato Soup, starchy sweet potatoes are cooked with aromatic onions and carrots and paired with salty Parmesan to balance the sweetness. A substantial amount of red chili adds fresh spice, further complementing the flavors. Topping the finished, velvety-smooth soup with toasted nuts excites the senses with a fun pop of texture. The delicately sweet, salty and spicy soup goes best with lighter, sweeter wines, such as Riesling or Rose.

PREP TIME: 10 minutes | **COOK TIME:** 35 minutes | **MAKES** about 4 servings

MEAL: Lunch, Dinner

2 tbsp (28 g) butter or ghee

1 large sweet onion, diced

2 large carrots, peeled and chopped

1 red chili pepper (or to taste), sliced, plus more for garnish (optional)

2–3 cloves garlic, minced or pressed

2-inch (5-cm) Parmesan rind (either Parmigiano-Reggiano or Grana Padano)

2–3 large sweet potatoes, peeled and chopped

5 cups (1.2 L) low-sodium vegetable broth

1 cup (100 g) Parmesan cheese (either Parmigiano-Reggiano or Grana Padano), finely grated, plus more for garnish

Sea salt and freshly ground black pepper, to taste

2 tbsp (8 g) fresh parsley, chopped, for garnishing

Toasted pine nuts or other nuts, coarsely chopped, for garnishing (optional)

1. In a large stockpot or Dutch oven, melt the butter over medium heat. Add the onion, carrots, chili (if using) and garlic. Sauté for 4 to 5 minutes.

2. Add in the Parmesan rind, sweet potatoes and broth. Stir well to combine and bring to a boil. Once boiling, reduce the heat to low and cover. Simmer for 28 to 30 minutes to infuse the broth with Parmesan flavor and until the sweet potatoes are very tender.

3. When done, carefully remove and discard the Parmesan rind.

4. Stir in the grated Parmesan. Using a hand blender, blend the soup until smooth. Alternatively, transfer the soup to a blender, working in batches, and blend until smooth. Taste the soup and season it with salt and pepper, as needed.

5. Ladle the soup into bowls and garnish with the Parmesan, parsley, chili slices and pine nuts, if using.

TIP: *Never ever throw away a Parmesan rind again. Save them in a resealable bag in your freezer. They'll give you the most flavorful broth. You can use them for any type of broth or soup, whether making it from scratch or when you want to enhance the flavor of a premade one.*

PARMESAN ROASTED CARROTS

Roasting carrots brings out all of their wonderful, natural sugars and the addition of grated, salty Parmesan is the best way to balance all of their caramelized sweetness. Beautifully colored rainbow carrots become even more vibrant after a trip to the oven, along with delicate fresh thyme leaves and minced garlic. Sprinkle the tray with lots of grated Parmesan and let it get nice and melty. The intensely sweet carrots and salty Parmesan make eating vegetables a whole lot easier in this side dish, especially when picky eaters are around. Pair with a dry Chenin Blanc to complement the sweetness of the caramelized carrots and saltiness of the Parmesan.

PREP TIME: 10 minutes | **COOK TIME:** 20 minutes | **MAKES** 6–8 servings

MEAL: Snack, Side Dish

2 lbs (907 g) rainbow carrots, peeled

2 cloves garlic, minced

2 tbsp (5 g) fresh thyme

3 tbsp (45 g) extra virgin olive oil

¾ tsp sea salt, or to taste

¼ tsp freshly ground black pepper, or to taste

4½ oz (128 g) Parmesan (either Parmigiano-Reggiano or Grana Padano), finely grated

1. Preheat the oven to 400°F (200°C). Line a large sheet pan (or two medium sheet pans) with parchment paper.

2. Using a sharp chef's knife, carefully trim and discard any unusable tops and bottoms from the carrots. Cut each carrot in half crosswise and then cut each half into thirds, lengthwise. Place the carrots in a large mixing bowl and add in the garlic, thyme, oil, salt and pepper. Toss well in the seasoning to coat evenly.

3. Layer the carrots on the prepared sheet pan, leaving some space between them, to ensure an even roast. Cook in the preheated oven for 10 minutes, or until almost tender.

4. Remove the tray from the oven and generously sprinkle the roasted carrots with the Parmesan. Return them to the oven and bake for 10 minutes longer, or until the cheese is melted and the carrots are tender and charred.

PARMESAN ROASTED CHICKPEA SALAD

Grated Parmesan becomes even more toasty and nutty when roasted with chickpeas in this fun Parmesan Roasted Chickpea Salad. Ordinary chickpeas become shatteringly crisp after some time in a hot oven while the salty Parmesan crisps and browns, coating the chickpeas with its flavorful glory. Delicious roasted asparagus and cherry tomatoes are added to the salad, along with a tart lemon vinaigrette for balancing the addictive chickpeas. No one will ever know that this salad is healthy. The crunchy, cheesy chickpeas are worthy of snacking on their own. The toasty flavors of the roasted chickpeas pair beautifully with buttery, dry Chardonnay.

PREP TIME: 15 minutes | **COOK TIME:** 30 minutes | **MAKES** 4 servings

MEAL: Lunch, Dinner

LEMON VINAIGRETTE

¼ cup (60 ml) freshly squeezed lemon juice

¼ cup (60 ml) extra virgin olive oil

2 tsp (10 ml) Dijon mustard

1 clove garlic, minced

1 tbsp (4 g) fresh parsley, minced

Sea salt and freshly ground black pepper, to taste

SALAD

14 oz (397 g) chickpeas, rinsed and drained

2 tbsp (30 ml) avocado or olive oil, divided

1 tsp garlic powder

1 tsp onion powder

½ tsp ground coriander seed

4½ oz (128 g) Parmesan (either Parmigiano-Reggiano or Grana Padano), finely grated, divided

10 oz (283 g) cherry or grape tomatoes

12–15 asparagus spears, cut into 1-inch (2.5-cm) pieces

Sea salt and freshly ground black pepper, to taste

1. Preheat the oven to 400°F (200°C). Line a large rimmed sheet pan with parchment paper or a silicone baking mat.

2. To make the lemon vinaigrette, in a small mixing bowl, whisk the lemon juice, olive oil, mustard, garlic and parsley until well combined. Season with salt and pepper, to taste.

3. Rinse and drain the chickpeas. Pat dry with paper towels. (This will make the chickpeas a bit crunchy. If you prefer them chewier, you can skip this step.)

4. In a large bowl, combine the chickpeas with 1 tablespoon (15 ml) of the avocado oil, garlic powder, onion powder, coriander seed and about three-fourths of the Parmesan. Toss well to evenly coat the chickpeas.

5. Spread the coated chickpeas in an even layer on the prepared sheet pan and transfer to the preheated oven. Roast for 15 to 20 minutes, or until the chickpeas begin to turn golden.

6. Meanwhile, in the same large bowl in which you mixed the chickpeas, add the tomatoes and asparagus. Sprinkle with the salt, pepper, reserved Parmesan and remaining 1 tablespoon (15 ml) of the avocado oil.

7. When the chickpeas are golden, carefully remove the pan from the oven. Stir once to mix and then gather them in the middle of the pan.

8. Arrange the tomatoes and asparagus around the gathered chickpeas. (Alternatively, you can use a second sheet pan.)

9. Return the pan to the oven and continue to roast for about 10 minutes, or until the tomatoes have burst and the asparagus is tender.

10. To serve the salad warm, as soon as you remove the pan from the oven, carefully add the roasted chickpeas, asparagus and tomatoes to a mixing bowl and toss with the dressing.

SPAGHETTI WITH PECORINO ROMANO, BLACK PEPPER AND NUTMEG

Spaghetti with Pecorino Romano and black pepper is one of the simplest dishes in Italian cuisine, and it's also one of the most flavorful, thanks to the pungent cheese and spicy, coarsely ground black pepper. As Pecorino Romano is the shining star in this dish, splurge for a higher-quality variety for the best results. Finely shredding the cheese with a microplane allows it to become part of the sauce and stick to every strand of pasta. Toasting the black pepper in olive oil, along with a grating of fresh nutmeg, enhances the spicy flavors. Tossing everything with a healthy pat of butter never hurts and tames the strong flavors of the tangy Pecorino and spicy pepper. Pair with a light-bodied red wine, such as Chianti or Pinot Noir.

PREP TIME: 10 minutes | **COOK TIME:** 12 minutes | **MAKES** about 6 servings

MEAL: Lunch, Dinner

1 whole nutmeg, or to taste

6½ oz (184 g) Pecorino Romano, plus more for garnish

1 tsp sea salt, or to taste

16 oz (454 g) spaghetti

2 cloves garlic, crushed

¼ cup (60 ml) extra virgin olive oil

1 tsp freshly ground black pepper

2 tbsp (28 g) butter

1. Start by grating the nutmeg and Pecorino Romano. Use a microplane or the smallest holes on a box grater for the finest yield.

2. Fill half of a large pot with water, season it with 1 teaspoon of salt and bring it to a boil. Add the pasta and garlic and cook until al dente, tender yet firm to the bite, according to the package directions. Drain the pasta and discard the garlic, reserving 1 cup (240 ml) of the cooking water.

3. In a large skillet, heat the oil over medium heat. Add in the freshly grated nutmeg and pepper, and cook for about 1 minute to release their flavors.

4. Stir in the butter, cooked pasta and the reserved pasta water. Sprinkle with the finely grated Pecorino Romano. Using tongs, toss the pasta while still on the heat.

5. Once the cheese is completely melted and the sauce is creamy, remove from the heat. Season with salt, to taste, and divide the pasta among the plates. Serve with the extra Pecorino Romano.

TIP: *Using less water when boiling the pasta will make the water starchier; this will help emulsify the sauce and bind it well to your pasta.*

BLACK PEPPER PECORINO AND MUSHROOM RISOTTO

Sharp Pecorino laced with bits of cracked black pepper gives this mushroom risotto a salty and spicy kick of flavor. Use a good mix of wild mushrooms for a variety of different flavors and textures. Be patient. Giving the mushrooms plenty of time to release their excess liquid allows them to brown and caramelize, giving the risotto a deeper flavor, especially with the sharp cheese. An important element of cooking risotto is to add the broth gradually and not all at once. When risotto is cooked slowly, the rice releases plenty of starch into the broth, resulting in a super-creamy mouthful without the use of heavy cream. Stir in the beautiful black pepper Pecorino at the end so it becomes nice and melty while retaining its sharp, intense flavor. Rice with cheese has never been yummier! This dish pairs best with lighter reds, such as Pinot Noir, or full-bodied whites, such as Chardonnay.

PREP TIME: 10 minutes | **COOK TIME:** 30 minutes | **MAKES** 5–6 servings
MEAL: Lunch, Dinner, Side Dish

1 tbsp (15 ml) olive oil

2 tbsp (28 g) butter

1 medium onion, finely chopped

8 oz (226 g) wild mushroom mix, larger pieces sliced, if needed

2 cloves garlic, finely chopped

¾ cup (180 ml) white wine

10½ oz (298 g) risotto rice, such as arborio

4 cups (960 ml) vegetable stock, used in batches

3½ oz (100 g) black pepper Pecorino, chopped

Small handful of curly fresh parsley leaves, chopped

1. In a shallow pan, heat the oil and butter over medium heat. Add the onion and sauté for about 5 minutes, or until soft.

2. Stir in the mushrooms and cook until they start to brown, 6 to 8 minutes. Add the garlic and white wine. Stir to combine. Allow the wine to bubble for 3 to 4 minutes, or until it fully reduces.

3. Stir in the rice and pour in 1 cup (240 ml) of the broth. Continue cooking over medium heat, simmering the rice and stirring often. When the rice has absorbed all of the liquid, add in another 1 cup (240 ml) of the broth. Continue to simmer and stir. Repeat until all of the broth has been used.

4. When done, the risotto should be plump, creamy and al dente. Taste, adjusting the seasonings if needed. If the rice is undercooked, add an extra splash of broth or hot water, and continue to simmer and stir until done.

5. Remove from the heat and stir in the black pepper Pecorino. Divide among bowls or plates and top with the parsley.

TIP: *If black pepper Pecorino is not easily available, use the regular Pecorino Romano found at any grocery store and just add some extra freshly ground pepper.*

MIX & MATCH

Delicious, Flavorful Combos of Different Cheeses and Textures

Sometimes it's hard to decide which cheese you want to use in a recipe. Do you want something rich and creamy or something dry and pungent? Well, guess what? You can use both! Combining cheeses is a great way to add multiple layers of flavor and texture to a dish. Think about the different types of cheese and what their strengths are, and use them accordingly.

As you've learned in previous chapters, you shouldn't feel as though you need to limit yourself to only one type of cheese. A great example of mixing and matching is in my recipe for Mediterranean Mozzarella Salad with Parmesan Dressing (page 129). Large chunks of mozzarella provide richness and creamy texture to the salad, while the tangy Parmesan dressing coats the fresh ingredients and flavors the salad throughout. Cheeseburger Crostini with Melted Emmental and Mozzarella (page 134) uses sliced mozzarella to give the dish a signature melty cheeseburger texture, while the Emmental melts on top and slightly browns for a more sophisticated touch.

In this chapter, we'll use everything we've learned about cheese to take it to the next level. True cheese lovers, like us, know that a good cheese shouldn't just be thrown into a dish. There is a time and place for each cheese, and you'll learn how to use them in combination with each other so that they can work in tandem. So, open your cheese drawer, pull out the grater and get ready for a saga of epically cheesy proportions.

MOZZARELLA ZUCCHINI FRITTATA WITH SHAVED PARMESAN

Nothing is better than a fresh, warm, cheesy frittata. Beaten eggs become beautifully puffed in the oven and this recipe includes sweet, summery zucchini, creamy mozzarella and salty Parmesan. The mozzarella creates a molten, cheesy center, while the Parmesan gives the frittata a delectably sharp, savory flavor. Serve alone or with a simple green salad for a healthy, yet craveable, light summer meal. This frittata pairs perfectly with a sparkling wine, such as Prosecco.

PREP TIME: 10 minutes | **COOK TIME:** 15–17 minutes | **MAKES** 6 servings

MEAL: Breakfast, Lunch, Dinner

12 large eggs

½ cup (120 ml) whole milk

Sea salt and freshly ground black pepper, to taste

4 oz (113 g) pancetta, diced

1 shallot, diced

2 cloves garlic, minced or pressed

1 tbsp (15 ml) red wine vinegar

1 large zucchini, chopped into bite-size pieces

1 tbsp (3 g) Italian seasoning

16 oz (454 g) fresh mozzarella cheese, drained and chopped into bite-size pieces

3 oz (85 g) Parmesan, shaved, plus more for garnishing

5 oz (142 g) cherry tomatoes, quartered, for garnishing

Small handful of fresh herbs of choice (e.g., oregano, basil, parsley or thyme), chopped, for garnishing

1. Preheat the oven to 350°F (180°C).

2. In a large bowl, beat the eggs with the milk and season with a pinch of salt and pepper. Set aside.

3. In a large, ovenproof skillet over medium heat, add the pancetta and cook for 4 to 5 minutes, or until it begins to brown.

4. Stir in the shallot and garlic. With a wooden spoon, sauté, stirring occasionally, for 3 to 4 minutes, or until the shallot is translucent. Pour in the vinegar and stir continuously for 1 to 2 minutes, scraping up any brown bits from the bottom of the skillet.

5. Add in the zucchini, Italian seasoning, salt and pepper. Continue to cook for 2 to 3 minutes, or until the zucchini starts to soften.

6. While the skillet is still over the heat, spread the vegetables in an even layer. Pour in the egg mixture. Evenly sprinkle the mozzarella cheese and Parmesan on top. Tilt the skillet to make sure the eggs settle evenly over the vegetables and cheese. Continue to cook for 1 to 2 minutes.

7. Once the eggs begin to set at the edges, transfer the skillet to the preheated oven. Bake for 8 to 12 minutes, or until the center is set.

8. Remove the frittata from the oven and allow it to cool for about 5 minutes. Cut into six slices. Garnish with the extra Parmesan, cherry tomatoes and herbs.

TIP: *To check your frittata for doneness, use a paring knife to make a small slit in the center of the frittata. If the eggs are still runny, bake for a few more minutes.*

MEDITERRANEAN MOZZARELLA SALAD WITH PARMESAN DRESSING

Adding fresh mozzarella pearls to salads is a great way to make them feel less like a healthy snack and more like a fun and hearty meal. The Parmesan dressing in this Mediterranean salad adds another punch of cheesy flavor with a vibrant kick from fresh lemon juice. The salad base contains a hefty portion of juicy mozzarella pearls, tangy marinated artichokes, sweet cherry tomatoes, fresh cucumber, red onion and briny olives. Toss it all with the creamy Parmesan dressing for a salad any cheese lover will adore. Serve with a full-bodied and citrusy Rousanne.

PREP TIME: 15 minutes | **MAKES** 4 servings

MEAL: Lunch, Dinner, Side Dish

PARMESAN DRESSING

2 tbsp (30 ml) lemon juice, freshly squeezed

1 tbsp (15 ml) apple cider vinegar

1 small clove garlic, minced

1 large pasteurized egg, yolk separated

1 tsp Italian herb seasoning

1 tsp Dijon mustard

¼ cup (25 g) Parmigiano-Reggiano, finely grated

¼ cup (60 ml) extra virgin olive oil

SALAD

8 oz (226 g) fresh mozzarella pearls or mini balls, drained

14 oz (397 g) marinated artichoke hearts, drained and quartered

10 oz (283 g) mixed cherry or grape tomatoes, halved

1 seedless cucumber, chopped

1 small red onion, thinly sliced

1 cup (180 g) black olives

Salt and freshly ground black pepper, to taste

1. To make the dressing, in a small bowl, add the lemon juice, vinegar, garlic, egg yolk, herb seasoning, mustard and Parmigiano-Reggiano. Whisk well, preferably with an electric whisk.

2. Slowly add in the oil and continue to whisk, until the dressing is smooth and emulsified. Refrigerate until ready to use.

3. In a large bowl, add the mozzarella pearls, artichoke hearts, tomatoes, cucumber, onion and olives.

4. Before serving, drizzle with the dressing and gently toss to evenly coat the salad. Season with salt and pepper, to taste.

SAVORY CHEESECAKE WITH HONEY-ROASTED PEARS

Cream cheese is oozing with versatility, as evidenced in this recipe for Savory Cheesecake with Honey-Roasted Pears. The cream cheese has a mild tang that works perfectly for playing with sweet flavors, such as caramelized pears. An addition of ricotta adds texture and gives the cheesecake some fluff—as it can often become dense. Salty feta and pungent Roquefort add complex savory notes. The oatmeal-cracker base makes this elegant appetizer a fancy version of the standard cheese-and-cracker fare. Serve with a sweet Chenin Blanc.

PREP TIME: 20 minutes | **COOK TIME:** 70 minutes | **MAKES** about 10 servings

MEAL: Snack, Appetizer, Dessert

BASE

4½ oz (128 g) oatmeal crackers, or other savory crackers of choice

¼ cup (57 g) salted butter, melted

FILLING

9 oz (255 g) full-fat cream cheese, at room temperature

9 oz (255 g) ricotta cheese

5½ oz (156 g) feta cheese, crumbled

2 large eggs, yolks separated, at room temperature

1 large egg, at room temperature

3½ oz (100 g) Roquefort, crumbled

HONEY-ROASTED PEARS

3 ripe pears (e.g., Bosc, Anjou or Concorde)

¼ cup (60 ml) honey

¼ tsp cinnamon, ground

½ tsp vanilla paste

TIP: *Homemade Ricotta Cheese (page 34) is perfect to use in this recipe.*

1. Adjust two oven racks, placing one in the lower-middle position and the other in the middle position. Preheat the oven to 320°F (160°C). Line a sheet pan with parchment paper and set it aside.

2. To make the base, place the crackers in a food processor and pulse into crumbs. Pour in the melted butter and continue to pulse until the crumbs are evenly coated. Transfer to a 7-inch (18-cm) springform pan. Press the crumbs into the bottom and up the sides to create the cheesecake base. Use the flat bottom of a cup or drinking glass to firmly pack the crust.

3. To make the filling, in a large mixing bowl, add the cream cheese, ricotta, feta, egg yolks and whole egg. Using a handheld or standard mixer, whisk until well combined. Add the Roquefort and, using a spatula, gently fold it into the filling mixture.

4. Pour the filling over the cracker base. Smooth to level it. Transfer to the lower middle rack of the oven and bake for 55 to 70 minutes, or until the cheesecake is golden with a slightly wobbly center.

5. To make the honey-roasted pears, slice the pears in half, lengthwise. Using a melon baller or small teaspoon, scoop out and discard the seeds. Place the pears on the prepared sheet pan, cut side up.

6. In a small bowl, add the honey, cinnamon and vanilla paste. Stir to combine. Spoon about half of the honey mixture over the pears and apply evenly. Transfer to the higher rack of the preheated oven. Roast for 35 to 40 minutes, or until the pears are tender, but not mushy, and golden on top.

7. When done, remove the cheesecake and roasted pears from the oven. Allow to cool for at least 2 hours. When ready to serve, top the cheesecake with the roasted pears and drizzle with the remaining honey mixture.

TRIPLE CHEESE GARLIC MUSHROOM TOAST

This Triple Cheese Garlic Mushroom Toast combines a triple threat of ooey-gooey Brie, pungent Gorgonzola and bold Pecorino for a perfectly balanced comfort food. Slices of hearty sourdough bread are topped with the melty yet full-flavored cheese combo before being toasted to crispy perfection. Sauté mixed wild mushrooms with a generous amount of minced garlic and acidic white wine, then top the gourmet cheese toast with the garlicky mushrooms for a cheesy appetizer that's not just for kids anymore. The three cheeses each bring something different to the party while balancing their strong flavors, allowing the meaty mushrooms to play a supporting role. When blending different cheeses, pair with something light and crisp, such as Sauvignon Blanc or Champagne.

PREP TIME: 10 minutes | **COOK TIME:** 10 minutes | **MAKES** 6 servings

MEAL: Breakfast, Lunch, Snack, Appetizer

⅓ cup (75 g) butter, at room temperature, divided

6 slices sourdough bread

6 oz (170 g) Gorgonzola, crumbled

8 oz (226 g) Brie, thinly sliced

12 oz (340 g) wild mushroom mix, larger pieces sliced, if needed

2 cloves garlic, peeled and minced

½ cup (120 ml) white wine

Sea salt and freshly ground black pepper, to taste

4 oz (113 g) Pecorino Romano, coarsely chopped

1 tbsp (4 g) fresh parsley, chopped

1. Preheat the oven to 400°F (200°C). Line a large sheet pan with parchment paper.

2. Spread the softened butter over the bread slices, reserving 1 tablespoon (14 g), and place them on the prepared sheet pan, butter side up. Top with the Gorgonzola and Brie.

3. Transfer to the oven and bake for 8 to 10 minutes, or until the cheese starts to melt and the edges begin to brown.

4. Meanwhile, in a cast-iron skillet, melt the reserved 1 tablespoon (14 g) of butter over medium-high heat. Add the mushrooms and fry, stirring occasionally, for 6 to 8 minutes, or until the mushrooms turn golden-brown. Stir in the garlic and wine. Continue to cook until all the liquid has evaporated. Season with salt and pepper, to taste. Remove from the heat.

5. Remove the tray from the oven and immediately spoon the sautéed mushrooms on top of the cheese toasts. Top with the Pecorino Romano and sprinkle with the parsley.

CHEESEBURGER CROSTINI WITH MELTED EMMENTAL AND MOZZARELLA

Cheeseburgers aren't just for fast food and summer barbecues anymore. Nutty Emmental and melty mozzarella pair up for these meaty, handheld morsels that are a gourmet version of the American classic. Complete with condiments, this cheeseburger crostini recipe proves that using old ingredients in new ways can be just as delicious as the original. Serve hot out of the oven for an epically cheesy burger experience with the crisp bite of toasted bread. Make sure to give yourself plenty of room for a nice, long cheesepull when digging into this comforting, cheesy appetizer. Try it with a light-bodied Beaujolais.

PREP TIME: 15 minutes | **COOK TIME:** 20 minutes | **MAKES** 8–10 servings

MEAL: Breakfast, Lunch, Appetizer

2 tsp (10 ml) olive oil

1 lb (454 g) 80/20 ground beef

2 tbsp (30 ml) Worcestershire sauce

1 tbsp (15 ml) Dijon mustard

¾ cup (59 g) tomatoes, diced with juices

½ tsp celery salt

½ tsp onion powder

Sea salt and freshly ground black pepper, to taste

1 crusty French loaf

Mayonnaise, as needed

10½ oz (298 g) mozzarella cheese, sliced

7 oz (198 g) Emmental, grated

½ small red onion, chopped

8–10 gherkins

1. Preheat the oven to 375°F (190°C). Line a large sheet pan with parchment paper.

2. Heat a large skillet over medium-high heat. Add the oil and beef. Cook for 4 to 5 minutes, or until the beef starts to brown, using a wooden spoon to break up the meat as it cooks.

3. Add the Worcestershire sauce, mustard, tomatoes, celery salt, onion powder, salt and pepper. Continue to cook, scrapping up any browned bits from the bottom of the skillet, for 2 to 3 minutes longer, or until the sauce has thickened.

4. Meanwhile, using a sharp bread knife, carefully slice the bread into ½-inch (1.3-cm)-thick slices.

5. Spread about 1 tablespoon (15 ml) of mayonnaise onto each slice of bread. Arrange the slices on the prepared sheet pan, mayonnaise side up. Top each with a slice of the mozzarella cheese followed by a large spoonful of the cooked beef. Sprinkle each with the Emmental and onion.

6. Transfer the sheet pan to the middle rack of the preheated oven. Bake for 10 to 12 minutes, or until the cheese is melted.

7. When done, remove from the oven and arrange the burgers on a platter. Spear a gherkin with a toothpick and insert it into the middle of a burger. Repeat with the remaining gherkins, using 1 for each crostini.

CHEESE MUSHROOM SKILLET

Covering mushrooms in cheese sauce is the perfect way to get kids to eat their vegetables. Salty, savory Parmesan and nutty, uber-melty Gruyère make a great combination for a gooey cheese sauce that is full of rich, cheesy flavor. The mushrooms are sautéed with garlic and white wine to add even more flavor and balance the bold cheese. Serve with a classic Malbec.

PREP TIME: 15 minutes | **COOK TIME:** 27 minutes | **MAKES** about 4 servings

MEAL: Lunch, Appetizer, Side Dish

3 tbsp (42 g) butter

4 cloves garlic, minced

2–3 fresh thyme sprigs, leaves picked

2 lbs (907 g) small button or Cremini mushrooms, cleaned

⅔ cup (160 ml) white wine

1¼ cups (300 ml) heavy cream

½ tsp paprika

Pinch of crushed red pepper flakes, to taste

Sea salt and freshly ground black pepper, to taste

2 oz (57 g) Parmesan, finely grated

6 oz (170 g) Gruyère, shredded

Small handful of fresh parsley, chopped, for garnishing

1. In a large skillet over medium heat, melt the butter. Add the garlic and thyme and cook for 1 minute, or until fragrant.

2. Add the mushrooms and sauté for 8 to 10 minutes, or until they start to brown and reduce in size.

3. Add the wine and continue to cook for 3 to 4 minutes, or until almost all the liquid has evaporated.

4. Stir in the heavy cream and bring to a boil. When the mixture starts boiling, immediately reduce the heat and simmer on low until the sauce thickens, for about 8 minutes.

5. Sprinkle with the paprika and red pepper flakes. Season with salt and pepper, to taste.

6. Stir in the Parmesan and Gruyère and continue to cook for about 5 minutes, or until the cheeses are melted and thoroughly incorporated into the sauce.

7. Garnish with the parsley and more red pepper flakes, if desired.

TIP: *Replace the white wine with vegetable broth, if needed.*

CHEDDAR AND FETA SPINACH MUFFINS

Salty feta and sharp Cheddar cheeses are the perfect pairing to bring a punch of flavor to these guilt-free double-cheese spinach muffins. Ground oats are a great way to make your favorite baked goods gluten-free. The addition of buttermilk provides tang and plays off the flavors of strong Cheddar and feta. A hefty amount of chopped spinach makes these muffins a treat that you can feel good about eating any time of the day. With cheesy flavor studded throughout the batter, you'll be craving these savory muffins in your sleep!

PREP TIME: 15 minutes | **COOK TIME:** 20 minutes | **MAKES** 12 muffins

MEAL: Breakfast, Lunch, Snack

6½ oz (184 g) frozen spinach, thawed

2 cups (250 g) oat flour (ground oats)

½ tbsp (7 g) baking powder

½ tsp baking soda

1 tsp onion powder

1 tsp garlic powder

¾ tsp sea salt, or to taste

½ tsp ground white pepper, or to taste

4 large eggs

1 cup (240 ml) buttermilk

2 tbsp (28 g) butter, melted

3 oz (85 g) sharp Cheddar, coarsely grated

6 oz (170 g) feta cheese, crumbled

1. Preheat the oven to 375°F (190°C). Line a twelve-cup muffin pan with individual cup liners.

2. Squeeze the thawed spinach in your hands to remove the excess water. Transfer to a chopping board. Using a sharp chef's knife, finely chop it.

3. In a large mixing bowl, add the flour, baking powder, baking soda, onion powder, garlic powder, salt and white pepper. Whisk until well combined.

4. In a second mixing bowl, beat the eggs with the buttermilk and melted butter. Slowly pour the egg mixture into the dry ingredients, beating constantly with a whisk until just incorporated.

5. Using a spatula, fold in the chopped spinach, Cheddar and feta cheeses. The batter should be thick with no visible lumps. Try not to overmix the batter to obtain fluffy, moist muffins.

6. Ladle the batter equally into the prepared muffin pan cups. Place the pan on the middle rack of the preheated oven.

7. Bake for 18 to 20 minutes, or until the muffins are golden and crusty on top, or until a toothpick inserted in the center comes out clean.

8. When done, remove from the oven and place on a rack to cool slightly before digging in!

DECONSTRUCTED CHEESE BOARD SALAD

The fruit-and-cheese board is a classic appetizer that gets a fun update in this beautiful, deconstructed cheese board salad. A cheese lover's paradise, this salad contains lightly dressed mixed greens that are topped with savory blue cheese, tangy goat cheese and buttery sheep's cheese. Caramelized onion chutney, sweet grapes and pecans give the salad just enough sweetness and crunch to offset the bold flavors of the cheeses. This salad is full of flavors that more sophisticated cheese lovers will appreciate. Try serving it with a Sangiovese-based wine, such as Rosso di Montalcino.

PREP TIME: 15 minutes | **MAKES** 4 servings

MEAL: Lunch, Appetizer, Dinner, Side Dish

4½ oz (128 g) mixed leafy greens

2 tbsp (30 ml) walnut oil

2 tbsp (30 ml) apple cider vinegar

Salt flakes and freshly ground black pepper, to taste

8 oz (226 g) white seedless grapes, halved

4½ oz (128 g) raw pecans, coarsely chopped

5 oz (142 g) Roquefort or any blue cheese of choice, crumbled or cubed

5 oz (142 g) goat cheese, crumbled or cubed

5 oz (142 g) sheep cheese, crumbled or cubed

2 tbsp (30 g) caramelized onion chutney

1. In a large bowl, add the greens and drizzle with the walnut oil and vinegar. Sprinkle with a pinch of the salt flakes and freshly ground pepper. Gently toss to combine.

2. Top the salad with the grapes, pecans, Roquefort, goat cheese and sheep cheese. Spoon the chutney on top.

THE CLASSIC CHEESE PLATTER

Cheese boards are a great way to show some creativity through food. Keep it simple but include a wide variety of seasonal cheeses, fruits and nuts. A good rule of thumb is to include one or two cheeses from each category of cheese except for fresh cheeses. While fresh cheeses have their place, they lose their integrity when included in cheese boards because they should be served chilled, rather than at room temperature. I've also included ideas for wine pairings, but feel free to adapt the wine choices based on your own taste and preferences. Not only is an epic cheese board easy to put together but, when artfully arranged, it makes a show-stopping appetizer as well. With this template for creating the perfect mix, you'll be able serve the perfect appetizer for your loved ones any time of the year.

PREP TIME: about 15 minutes | **YIELD VARIES**

MEAL: Snack, Appetizer

Cheese List

FIRM AND SEMI-FIRM CHEESES

Pecorino Romano, Pecorino Toscano, Grana Padano, Bianco Sardo, Cheddar, Gouda, Gruyère, Emmental, Asiago, Manchego, Abondance, hard goat cheese

SOFT AND BUTTERY CHEESES

Brie, Camembert, Goat Cheese, Cremeux des Citeaux, Finn, Cremeux de Bourgogne, Coulommiers, Muenster

BLUE-VEINED AND FUDGY CHEESES

Stilton, Roquefort, Gorgonzola Dolce or Piccante, Danish Blue, Devon Blue, Bay Blue, Blu Brie, Blue di Bufala, Bleu de Bresse

Accompaniments

CRACKERS OR BREADS

Plain, whole grain, oatmeal, sesame crackers; mini rye toasts; breadsticks; Chili Grana Padano Biscuits (page 112)

FRESH FRUITS

Apples, pears, figs, berries

DRIED FRUITS

Apricots, dates, figs, apples, cranberries

NUTS

Walnuts, pecans, almonds, cashews, pistachios

PICKLES

Cornichons, baby carrots, radishes, piri-piri, artichokes, caperberries

OLIVES

Green, black, kalamata, stuffed olives

CHUTNEYS, HONEY, JAMS AND OTHER PRESERVES

Mango, pear or apple chutney; raw honey; fig jam; onion or sweet pickle relish

Wine Suggestions

SEMI-FIRM AND FIRM CHEESES

These cheeses go well with a medium-bodied red such as a Cabernet Sauvignon or a Rioja. Or if your budget allows, you can never go wrong with a bold age-worthy Brunello Di Montalcino.

SOFT AND BUTTERY CHEESES

These go well with fruity red wines such as Beaujolais or Sangiovese. A floral, dry Rose Lambrusco would be nice, too.

BLUE-VEINED CHEESES

Always pair blue cheese with red wines! Sauternes is the classic pairing for Roquefort; Stilton pairs great with a complex Port; and Gorgonzola pairs well with a drier style of Marsala.

(continued)

THE CLASSIC CHEESE PLATTER (CONTINUED)

1. Choose three to five different cheeses to add to your board.

    Cheeses can be named and categorized in many ways. To make your life easier, use the cheese list I've made for you with the most popular ones. Just mix and match to include both hard and soft varieties and definitely add some blue-veined cheeses to add texture and diversity to your board.

    You'll want everyone to find at least one type of cheese they love, so you can't go wrong with choosing any from the list. Once you've decided on the cheeses, the rest will be fairly simple.

    Depending on how many people you will be serving, you can use about 3 ounces (85 g) of cheese in total per person. If you serve a platter as a starter, then reduce the amount to about 1½ ounces (43 g) of cheese per person.

2. Find a large platter or slate and arrange the cheeses on it. Slice one type of cheese thinly, then cube another and leave others whole. This way, you'll have different shapes that will look more attractive. When arranging the cheeses, leave plenty of space in between.

3. Next, add in the accompaniments. Be creative, and try to include something fresh, sweet, salty and tangy to go with the cheeses. Start by adding and arranging pieces that require more space, such as a bunch of grapes, a row of crackers or pinch bowls.

4. Finish your board by filling in the empty spaces. Use the smaller-sized accompaniments—nuts, cranberries and fresh berries—to fill any spaces left on your board.

    See? Easy peasy, fun and cheesy! Don't forget to keep the plate refrigerated until ready to serve.

5. When ready to serve, place your masterpiece platter in the center of the table, along with some fancy cheese knives.

6. Oh, wait. Don't forget to chill or breathe the wine!

TIP: *Cheese platters are ideally served at room temperature. Before eating, place the tray on the table for 30 minutes to bring out the best flavors.*

CHEESE LIST

FRESH (PAGE 13)

American Neufchâtel
Chevre Log
Cotija
Cream Cheese
Curd Cheese
Farmer Cheese
Fromage Blanc
Goat Curd
Labneh
Mascarpone
Mozzarella
Queso Fresco
Ricotta

SOFT (PAGE 39)

Brie
Cambozola
Camembert
Chaource
Cottage Cheese
Feta
French Neufchâtel
Gorgonzola
Muenster (American version)
Munster (French version)
Tommes

SEMI-SOFT (PAGE 67)

American
Chaumes
Colby Jack
Danish Blue
Danish Fontina
Halloumi
Havarti

Jarlsberg
Pepper Jack
Port Salut
Reblochon
Roquefort
Saint Nectaire
Stilton

SEMI-FIRM (PAGE 89)

Abbaye
Abondance
Cheddar
Colby
Comté
Danish Feta
Edam
Emmental
Gouda
Gruyère
Monterey Jack
Provolone
Raclette
Swiss

FIRM (PAGE 107)

Aged Cheddar
Aged Gouda
Asiago
Beaufort
Cheshire
Grana Padano
Gruyère
Manchego
Parmesan
Pecorino

ACKNOWLEDGMENTS

A huge thanks to all the readers and followers of Blondelish.com. Without your amazing support and encouragement, this book—and my website—would not exist.

I am also deeply grateful to Sarah Monroe and the amazing team at Page Street Publishing for giving me this opportunity. Writing a recipe book has always been my dream. Thank you for helping me turn my dream into reality.

Special thanks go to my husband, who has been by my side throughout this journey. He was invaluable in helping me put this book together.

Last, but not least, I'd like to thank you, the reader, for trying out my recipes. I hope you enjoy them as much as I do. If you know other cheese lovers, please share these recipes with them. I'm sure you'll be making their day.

ABOUT THE AUTHOR

Mihaela Metaxa-Albu is a recipe author and former chef from London. She previously worked as a pastry chef at Zuma and Ottolenghi, two of London's finest and most exclusive restaurants. After building experience in the culinary world of the British capital, she created her own recipe website, Blondelish.com.

Blondelish combines Mihaela's skills in photography, videography and the culinary arts, providing her readers with healthy recipes that are easy to make, requiring nothing more than some basic cooking skills, quick preparation and affordable ingredients.

She is also an entrepreneur, selling kitchenware, utensils and, as you would expect, cheese boards, under her own brand. Visit her online store, blauke.com, to find some of the cooking tools used in this book's recipes and photos.

INDEX